P R E F A C E

The subject I'm about to present in the pages of this book is far too large to handle in the few pages that I've assigned to it. At best, this book will be a mere survey of a key thread that ties sacred history together. Many, many good books have been written on this subject, and once you've flown over the landscape of this material, you might want to put your feet on the ground and read some of the books listed in the bibliography, some of which are more comprehensive on the subject than this one.

So why do I bother writing at all if there are better books on the subject? It's simple. I have found this material so fascinating that every fiber of my being wants to *say something* about it. Is there an extra-human presence on planet earth? Yes. And it's closer than you might think.

With the unpleasant reports we witness every night on the evening news, many people are now clinging desperately to the guardrail of life, hoping merely to survive. Their teeth are clenched and their knuckles are white. If they could only understand that there is a Presence in this world in control of what ultimately happens, they would breathe a sigh of relief.

This book is dedicated to the millions of people out there who desperately need to discover the Presence in their own lives.

CLOSER THAN YOU THINK

THE PRESENCE

*To my friend + sister in Christ
Love Kelly Miller*

SHAWN BOONSTRA

IT IS WRITTEN
INTERNATIONAL TELEVISION

and Pacific Press Publishing Association

Book Design and Layout by Fred Knopper
Cover Design and Illustrations by Palmer Halvorson
Editing by Judy Knopper and Kari Kurti
Photo credit: www.photos.com

Additional copies of this book are available by
calling toll free 1-888-664-5573 or visiting
www.itiswritten.com

Printed in the United States of America
by Pacific Press Publishing Association
Nampa, Idaho / Oshawa, Ontario, Canada
www.pacificpress.com

ISBN 10: 0-8163-2175-2
ISBN 13: 978-0-8163-2175-9

Contents

PROLOGUE

The ancient Philistines had had enough. What had started as an impressive military victory had turned into a living nightmare. The land was teeming with rodents and a strange painful plague was beleaguering its occupants. Five kings gathered for a conference. There was only one thing left to do: return the Ark of the Covenant to the children of Israel.

For many of the ancient peoples who were accustomed to worshiping statues, the Ark that the Israelites carried with them into Canaan was not merely a religious symbol. It was, in their way of thinking, a god in itself. And so when the Philistines managed to capture the Ark in battle, they were ecstatic. They placed it in the temple of the fish god, Dagon, in the city of Ashdod—as tangible proof that the god of the Philistines was greater than the God of the Israelites.

Early the next morning, when they went into the temple to admire the spoils of war, something very troubling had happened. Unseen hands had pushed the statue of Dagon over on its face in front of the Ark, as if the pagan god were worshiping the God of Israel. Horrified, they set the statue back up in its place. The next morning, when they came back to check on it, something far worse had happened: this time the statue was lying on the threshold of the temple, with its head and hands broken off. The event was so traumatic for the priests of Dagon that for years to come, they refused to step on the threshold of the temple where their god had suffered such humiliation.

Then the problem spread from the temple of Dagon into the rest of the land. A strange plague of painful tumors began to sweep through the country, and the troublesome Ark was desperately moved from one city to the next, until it came to rest in Ekron, where scores of people mysteriously died. What had seemed like a valuable acquisition (after all, the Israelites had formerly been in the habit of carrying the Ark into battle and winning) suddenly became the scourge of the land, and they decided to send it home.

The Ark was loaded onto a cart drawn by cows that had been separated from their calves. This was done deliberately, because the Philistines knew that cows with calves would naturally want to return to their young instead of wandering great distances. If the cows headed for Israelite territory instead of returning home, the Philistines would know that a Deity greater than Dagon was at work. An offering of gold, meant to appease the God of Israel, was also loaded on the ark.

Scarcely daring to watch, they set the cows free—and immediately they knew their hunch was right. The untended cows headed straight for Israelite territory, without so much as wavering to the right or left.

The strange story does not end there. The biblical record tells us that the Ark of the Covenant came to rest in a field in Bethshemesh. Reapers working the fields were overjoyed to see the Ark miraculously returned to them seven months after it had been captured. Foolishly, they did something that even the Philistines hadn't dared to do: they lifted the lid of the Ark to look inside. Scores of them died as a result.[1]

Twenty years later, as the Ark was being moved to a more permanent home, the oxen that were pulling the cart stumbled, and one man reached out to touch the Ark so that it wouldn't fall off the cart. He died instantly.

For most of its existence, the Ark of the Covenant was kept out of human sight, behind a thick veil in the innermost part of the Hebrew sanctuary. Everybody—including the neighboring countries—knew there was something special about it. If you touched it, you would die. If you treated it with disregard, terrible things would happen.

What was so extraordinary about this mysterious golden chest? What is the ancient secret of the Ark of the Covenant? Where is it today? Why was it so important? Keep reading. The story is absolutely remarkable. It has something of great consequence to say to our twenty-first century world.

---

[1] There are differing opinions as to how many died. The syntax of the original Hebrew makes it difficult to tell whether 50,070 people died, or 70 people out of 50,000 died. Some scholars believe the word translated "thousand" would be better translated "family," which would mean that 70 men from 50 families died. Most biblical scholars agree that the death toll was seventy.

The Fingerprints of God

At the beginning of the 13th century, a mathematician by the name of Leonardo Pisano studied a problem that had a revolutionary solution. It went something like this: "A certain man put a pair of rabbits in a place surrounded on all sides by a wall. How many pairs of rabbits can be produced from that pair in a year if it is supposed that every month each pair begets a new pair, which from the second month on becomes productive?"

On paper, Leonardo listed the number of rabbits at the end of each month, and came up with the following numerical sequence:

$$0, 1, 1, 2, 3, 5, 8, 13, 21, 34, 55...$$

It proved to be more than a simple math problem. Those numbers have come to be known as the *Fibonacci numbers*.[2] They hold some very interesting properties, including the fact that each number in the series is the sum of the two numbers before it.

As strange as it might seem, that sequence of numbers might just hold the key to a very important secret of the universe. Students of the Fibonacci numbers have noticed that each number bears a special relationship to the numbers surrounding it. After the first few numbers, the ratio of any Fibonacci number to the one before it is approximately

1.618:1. And the ratio of any Fibonacci number to the one after it, surprisingly, is about 0.618:1.

Of course, for those who don't find mathematics fascinating, the question is, "so what?" Well, as it turns out, that ratio is very special. It is so special, in fact, that it is called the "golden ratio," and there is a growing group of devotees who are studying it. They have even given this remarkable number a name: *phi*.

When a line has been segmented into this ratio, it has special properties:

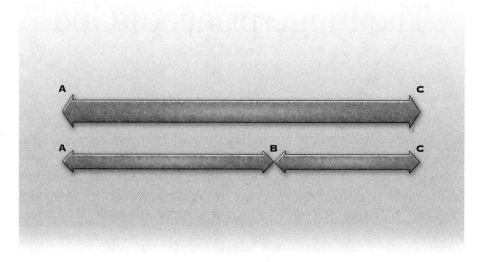

The Golden Ratio

If you use the golden ratio to divide the line AC, you get two pieces, AB and BC. (And you thought you would never use your high-school math again!) The ratio between AC and AB is 1.618034, and the ratio between AB and BC is exactly the same!

Again, so what? Stay with me for a moment, because this proves to be really important. Mathematicians have applied this special ratio to a number of geometrical shapes. If a rectangle is 1.618 times as long as it is wide, it is known as a *golden rectangle*. Likewise, if a triangle is 1.618 times high as it is wide, it is known as a *golden triangle:*

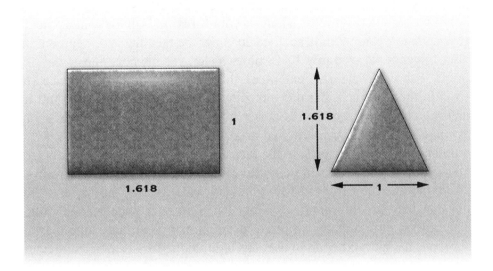

A golden rectangle and golden triangle.

Students of this special ratio have discovered these proportions in just about every piece of art or architecture that human beings consider beautiful—particularly in great works of art that have stood the test of time. For example, some believe the dimensions of the Parthenon in Greece to be based on this ratio. Others have noticed that Leonardo Da Vinci seems to have used this proportion in many of his sketches. Even the face of the Mona Lisa seems to fit inside a golden rectangle, since it is approximately 1.618 times as high as it is wide! Many other notable Renaissance painters also used this ratio to create the masterpieces that still hang in prestigious museums to this day.

The question, of course, is *why*? Why did our ancestors find this ratio to be so beautiful?

The answer is startling for a world that has become convinced that the earth came into existence through some sort of cosmic accident billions of years ago. The great architects and artists that used this ratio so freely appear to have been mimicking proportions that occur frequently in nature. It may in fact be one of the blueprints used to structure the universe we live in.

Consider the fact that your forearm is approximately 1.618 times as long as your hand, and the span from your fingertips to your elbow is approximately 1.618 times as long as your forearm. Is that a coincidence? If you are tempted to think so, then consider the fact that each segment in your finger is also roughly 1.618 times as long as the next one.

If that were the full extent of this ratio's natural occurrence, it wouldn't mean much, but this amazing number surfaces so often in the natural world that it demands closer investigation. The human face, on average, is roughly proportioned according to the golden ratio. Take a moment some time to analyze the faces of people the world considers to be strikingly beautiful, and you will notice something really interesting. Their mouths tend to be 1.618 times as wide as their noses, and the distance between their pupils is about 1.618 times as wide as the mouth. The golden ratio appears so often in the human face that some plastic surgeons have even begun to use it as a guideline for cosmetic surgery.

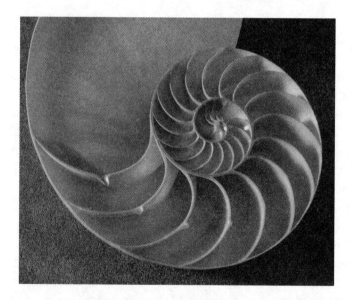

If you create a spiral based on Fibonacci numbers, where every quarter turn is 1.618 times as far from the center as the previous one, you get what is known as a *golden spiral*. Amazingly, most of the spirals found in nature are golden spirals. The shells of a nautilus or a snail, for example, are both golden spirals. So are hurricanes, ram's horns, the tails of seahorses, the cochlea of the human ear, whirlpools in the ocean, the seed patterns of sunflowers and pinecones, and the tail of a comet as it winds around the sun.

Perhaps you have noticed, as you look at the seeds in a sunflower, that there are actually two sets of spirals: one running clockwise, and the other running counterclockwise. These are generally golden spirals, and the number of spirals running in each direction is never the same. There might be eight spirals running in one direction, and thirteen in the other. Furthermore, the number of spirals running in either direction will be numbers from the Fibonacci sequence, and will usually be neighboring numbers from the sequence!

The list of golden ratios found in nature is nearly inexhaustible. If you create ratios between the lengths of years on neighboring planets in our solar system, they seem to be Fibonacci numbers. A strand of DNA appears to be a twisted stack of golden rectangles. It also appears in music, the proportions of a dolphin's body, and much, much more.

One natural occurrence that might not be immediately obvious is the arrangement of leaves along the branches of many trees and plants. In a large number of plants, each successive leaf will grow out of the branch at approximately 137.5 degrees from the previous leaf. In other words, the leaves *spiral* around the branch, and if you draw that same angle (137.5 degrees) inside a circle, you end up with two arcs that are proportioned according to the golden ratio. The longest arc is—you guessed it—1.618 times as long as the shortest one.

It this all a coincidence?

Over the last couple of centuries, many have managed to convince themselves that the world is a product of mere chance, which would leave us with the very real possibility that we are alone in the universe. As a devastating sense of helplessness and futility washes across the planet, many are beginning to sense that our ancestors knew something that we have forgotten. Somehow, they were more in touch. They seemed to have contact with something—or somebody—that was outside of our day-to-day human existence. As a result, they had greater peace of mind.

Are we really alone in the universe? The numbers tell a different story. The more we study the world, the more we are forced back to the conclusion that our existence is not an accident. What science once spurned as superstition is receiving new attention. Robert Jastrow, the renowned astronomer, puts it like this:

For the scientist who has lived by his faith in the power of reason, the story ends like a bad dream. He has scaled the mountains of ignorance; he is about to conquer the highest peak; as he pulls himself over the final rock, he is greeted by a band of theologians who have been sitting there for centuries.[3]

We are starting to discover that in spite of colossal advances in our collective body of knowledge, we still don't have all the answers. Those who were spurned as superstitious and backwards in the last century for being religious are starting to find themselves vindicated by the numbers. There really *is* more than first meets the eye in this universe. If you pay careful attention to the fingerprints that Someone has left all over the surface of the planet, they provide mounting evidence of a Presence in this world that exists quite apart from us. That Presence has left other startling evidence as well.

---

[2] "Fibonacci" was apparently a nickname for Leonardo Pisano.

[3] Jastrow, R., *God and the Astronomers,* (New York: W.W. Norton, 1978) p. 116

CHAPTER TWO

The Presence

A little girl was forced to spend the night in an underground air raid shelter during of the heat of battle in World War II. Her father gently tucked her into her cot, kissed her on the forehead, and then turned out the light. Carefully, he made his way to his own bed on the other side of the concrete bunker.

It was not a good night for sleeping. The little girl's cot shook each time a bomb fell on the city above. Even though she was very young, she was acutely aware of the horrors outside her shelter. Her own mother had been killed during another attack.

Her stomach was in a knot; it was impossible to sleep. The smothering darkness was terrifying. She closed her eyes, clutched her favorite rag doll, and tried to be brave. Sheer terror quickly broke her resolve. In a hoarse whisper, she called out: "Daddy! Are you there?"

Back through the darkness her father's voice came to her, calm and steady. "Yes, honey, Daddy's right here. Everything's going to be fine. Please—close your eyes and go to sleep now."

"Yes, Daddy."

She pulled the blankets up past her chin and tried to peer through the blackness in her father's direction. It was impossible to see anything, so she pinched her eyes shut and desperately tried to sleep; but of course, the effort of *trying* to sleep robs you of any chance of achieving it. She waited for what seemed like an appropriate number of minutes and then cried out again: "Daddy, are you *still* there?"

"Yes, sweetheart. I'm still here, and everything's going to be okay. Now please, get some sleep; in the morning, everything will be a lot better."

It was reassuring to hear her father's voice again. She felt a little better for a moment, but then the darkness pushed her helplessly to the edge of fear's precipice. Another explosion rocked the shelter, and she called out, terrified.

"*Daddy?*"

"Yes, honey. What is it?"

"Daddy, just one more thing. I was wondering..."

She fell silent for a moment, as if afraid to ask.

"What is it?" Her father's voice was patient and understanding.

"Daddy, I was just wondering if your face is turned my way."

A smile crept across her father's face. It was the first opportunity he'd had to smile since he had lost his wife.

"Yes," he said softly, "my face is turned your way."

With a renewed sense of confidence, the young girl fell asleep. She knew her father was watching her.

Adam stood at the end of the garden and leaned on his hand-made hoe. A heavy bead of sweat ran down over his eyebrows, stinging his eyes. He wiped his face with the back of his hand, and then wiped his hand on his clothes. His palm was raw and blistered from the handles of his rough gardening tools. He noticed a small thorn poking through the skin just below his thumb. As he pulled it out, he suddenly felt his stomach tighten.

How could I do it? he thought. *How could I just throw away everything I had for this?*

He glanced back over his shoulder in the direction of Eden, and another wave of anxiety squeezed the pit of his stomach. Not only was he banned from that place, his descendants would be barred from it, too. One day, when his children and grandchildren were old enough to notice the hardships and disappointments of life, he was going to have to explain why they were not permitted to live in the Garden. He turned back to his work. The new garden was nothing like the old one. He bent over and scooped up a handful of dirt, letting some of it trickle through his fingers. Instead of living forever, he was going back to *that*. Eventually, his children would have to turn over the soil, not to plant a garden, but to prepare a *grave*.

For dust you are, and to dust you shall return. The words still haunted him. He already knew just how true they were, because he had been faced with the horrific reality of committing the limp body of his son to the ground. His own child had become the first human victim of his rebellion against God.

A tear trickled down his cheek as he remembered the joy that Abel had brought him, and his heart ached to see his son again. What made it nearly impossible to think about was the fact that he knew he was personally responsible for every bit of suffering that the world would have to endure. He had set in motion the circumstances that would yield heartache for thousands of years to come.

Almost overcome with anguish, Adam looked back at Eden and suddenly saw a brilliant flash of light near the gates. The sick feeling in his stomach quickly subsided. *That's right,* he thought. *It's not over yet. God's face is still turned my way.*

A small smile pushed at the corners of his mouth as hope swelled in his heart, and with a new sense of contentment, he turned back to his work.

Of course, I don't know for sure that anything like that ever actually happened outside the gates of the Garden of Eden, but it's not unlikely. Adam must have done a lot of hard thinking in the days and months after his expulsion from the Garden. Imagine the tragic contrast between Paradise and the deteriorating world outside its gates. What was it like to face a world you had personally destroyed?

What was it like for Adam when God arrived in the Garden that first evening after he sinned? What was it like for him to feel his heart pounding wildly in his chest in a state of crippling fear—for the very first time? Or to find it necessary to *hide* for the first time in human history?

And they heard the sound of the LORD God walking in the garden in the cool of the day, and Adam and his wife hid themselves from the presence of the LORD God among the trees of the garden. Then the LORD God called to Adam and said to him, "Where are you?" So he said, "I heard Your voice in the garden, and I was afraid because I was naked; and I hid myself." (Genesis 3:8-10)

Nakedness, of course, was just an excuse to hide from God. Before the fig-leaf apron, Adam had never worn any real clothing. Adam hadn't thrown away his clothes; he had thrown away his spotless relationship with God. He had thrown away the cloak of glory and righteousness God had clothed him with at creation. His joy was gone because he had been unfaithful to God. He felt like a guilty spouse on the drive home from a sordid affair. That's why he hid from God.

Hiding in the trees, of course, was pointless. God knew exactly where he was, because it is impossible to escape His presence:

Where can I go from Your Spirit? Or where can I flee from Your presence? If I ascend into heaven, You are there; if I make my bed in hell, behold, You are there. If I take the wings of the morning, and dwell in the uttermost parts of the sea, even there Your hand shall lead me, and Your right hand shall hold me. If I say, "Surely the darkness shall fall on me," even the night shall be light about me; indeed, the darkness shall not hide from You, but the night shines as the day; the darkness and the light are both alike to You. (Psalm 139:7-12)

The post-sin encounter between God and Adam is one of the most important passages in the Bible, because it reveals something important about the nature of God. The Creator would have been well within His rights to eradicate our first parents from the face of the earth, but instead, He chose to redeem them. With tears in His voice He calls out: "Adam, where are you?"

Why did God ask this question? As the all-knowing God, He could easily see Adam cowering in the bushes. God's question was a tortured lament over the family that had just been fragmented. Looking down through the corridors of time, He could already see every heartbreaking funeral that would take place because of human rebellion. He could see the sickness, pain, poverty, loneliness and crime that would plague our lives. He could see a human race tragically cut off from the direct presence of their Heavenly Father.

Years later, the prophet Isaiah wrote this about the effects of sin on our lives:

But your iniquities have separated you from your God; and your sins have hidden His face from you, so that He will not hear. (Isaiah 59:2)

Sin creates a significant barrier between the human race and God. He simply cannot allow it to dwell in His perfect and holy presence. If He were to allow sin to continue in His presence without responding to it, He would cease to be a loving and merciful God. Suffering is not part of His original plan for the universe. Even though it tore at the heart of God, the original pair had to be expelled from the Garden.

Adam and Eve were ushered out of Paradise into a life awash with heartache and hardship. But as the gates of Eden swung shut behind them, God did not close the door on hope. He left us with the promise of full restoration:

And I will put enmity between you and the woman, and between your seed and her Seed; He shall bruise your head, and you shall bruise His heel. (Genesis 3:15)

Speaking to the serpent that deceived Eve, God declared that Someone would come from the human race Who would crush the serpent's head and restore the human race to perfect communion with God. Then, in addition to this first Messianic promise, God established a presence at the gates of the Garden:

So He drove out the man; and He placed cherubim at the east of the garden of Eden, and a flaming sword which turned every way, to guard the way to the tree of life. (Genesis 3:24)

With the same breath that mentions the expulsion of Adam from the Garden, the Bible tells us that God instituted a tangible presence for Himself on a sinful planet. Through it, He was sending Adam a very important message: even in our rebellion, the heart of God still aches to be with us. Even though sin creates a significant barrier, God does everything possible to maintain His relationship with us. The human race could see cherubs at the edge of the Garden—a symbol of hope. The gates to Eden would not be closed forever. The damaged connection between the Creator and the created would be completely healed, and we would safely dwell in the presence of God again.

Take a close look at Genesis 3:24, because there is more to this passage than first meets the eye. It says that God "placed" angels east of Eden. The Hebrew word in the original text is *shakan*, which literally means "to cause to dwell." In other words, God didn't simply *locate* angels and a flaming sword by the Garden; He caused them to *dwell* there.

The wording is significant, because of what the Bible teaches us about cherubim. They are not the little winged babies made popular by the greeting card industry. Cherubim are an angelic order that holds some of the highest positions in heaven. In his amazing book, *With Jesus in His Sanctuary,* Dr. Leslie Hardinge makes the following observation:

G. Bramley long ago suggested that the initial Hebrew letter of cherub (k) means "like," and that its second syllable (rb) signifies one "great in power, in wisdom and glory, or whatever can be termed perfection" (Philalethes, The Cherubim of Glory). It is the root of "rabbi," and may be applied to God. The term cherub, therefore, describes one "who is like the divine majesty," and focuses on his character.[4]

Cherubs, far from being babies with wings, are among the loftiest creatures in the universe. They perform important tasks and hold powerful positions. This is the position that Lucifer himself held before he rebelled against God:

"You were the anointed cherub who covers; I established you; you were on the holy mountain of God; you walked back and forth in the midst of fiery stones." (Ezekiel 28:14)

Lucifer was a "covering" cherub, which is an angel that stands right next to the throne of God and covers it with his wings. The presence of cherubs in a passage of the Bible is a clear signal to the reader to look for the presence of God. In fact, God is often described as the One who "dwells between the cherubim:"

Give ear, O Shepherd of Israel, You who lead Joseph like a flock; You who dwell between the cherubim, shine forth! (Psalm 80:1)

The LORD reigns; let the peoples tremble! He dwells between the cherubim; let the earth be moved! (Psalm 99:1)

Then Hezekiah prayed to the LORD, saying: "O LORD of hosts, God of Israel, the One who dwells between the cherubim, You are God, You alone, of all the kingdoms of the earth. You have made heaven and earth." (Isaiah 37:15, 16)

Two cherubim, whose wings "covered" the top of the Ark (known as the "mercy seat"), also graced the Ark of the Covenant. We will spend more time on the Ark in a later chapter, but for now it is interesting to note that in the camp of Israel the presence of God would appear between the two golden cherubim above the Ark:

"And the cherubim shall stretch out their wings above, covering the mercy seat with their wings, and they shall face one another; the faces of the cherubim shall be toward the mercy seat. You shall put the mercy seat on top of the ark, and in the ark you shall put the Testimony that I will give you. And there I will meet with you, and I will speak with you from above the mercy seat, from between the two cherubim which are on the ark of the Testimony, about everything which I will give you in commandment to the children of Israel." (Exodus 25:20-22)

The presence of cherubim signal the presence of God, especially when you have something "shining" in between them. Add to this the fact that fire is often used in the Bible as a symbol of the presence of God,[5] and an interesting picture begins to unfold outside of the gates of Eden. Is it possible that the cherubs and the fiery sword were actually a manifestation of the presence of God Himself?

Dr. Leslie Hardinge makes the following important observation:

The Lord "placed" (shakan) the cherubim at the east of Eden. This word springs from the same root as does shekinah, the visible manifestation of Deity (Gen 3:24). The Septuagint (LXX) used a Greek term (tasso) to stress that God arranged them in a well-ordered setting. Near his death Moses reminded Israel that it was "the Good Will of Him that dwelt (shakan) in the bush" (Deut 33:16) Who had summoned him to service. "Dwelt" might be rendered as placed His Shekinah or abode in a tent of light. It depicts the radiant Christ concealed in the incandescent desert shrub. In describing His incarnation, John used a term which is probably a Helenized form (skene) of shekinah (from shakan; cf. John 1:14), both have the same three consonants skn) to represent Christ's Divinity tabernacling or "tenting" in humanity.[6]

Shekinah is a word specifically used to describe the glorious presence of God. It emphasizes God's desire to dwell among His people. When the Bible says that God caused two angels with bright flaming swords to "dwell" at the gates of Eden, it is a clear signal that the presence of God was established there. Calvinist Bible scholar Hugh Martin noticed this important biblical detail several hundred years ago:

...for the primitive worship which immediately succeeded the fall,

some special locality was consecrated as the place where Jehovah's name was placed; where His worshippers assembled: to which they brought their offerings, that they might call upon His name through sacrifice, and receive tokens of their acceptance, and fresh intimations, it may be, or the Lord's will. Most probably, in the days of the first family of our race, the gate of the garden of Eden, where God placed the cherubims and the flaming sword, constituted the seat of sacred worship; occupying the place and serving the purpose which, in after generations, were occupied and served by the tabernacle in the wilderness and in Shiloh, and ultimately by the temple, on Mount Moriah.[7]

Famed Bible scholars Jamieson, Fausset and Brown said this about the mysterious passage at the end of the third chapter of Genesis:

The passage should be rendered thus: "And he dwelt between the cherubim at the East of the Garden of Eden and a fierce fire, or Shekinah, unfolding itself to preserve the way of the tree of life." This was the mode of worship now established to show God's anger at sin and teach the mediation of a promised Saviour as the way of life, as well as of access to God. They were the same figures as were afterwards in the tabernacle and temple; and now, as then, God said, "I will commune with thee from above the mercy seat, from between the two cherubims."[8]

There was a Presence established at the gates of Eden as a powerful reminder that God had not abandoned the human race in spite of our rebellion against Him. The way to the Tree of Life had been closed, but only for the time being. One day, because of a remarkable plan worked out by the Ancient of Days even before the world was created, man would once again commune with God face to face. In the darkness of despair, as the human race began to sink in suffering, sin and death, Adam could still look over at the gates of the Garden and see it for himself: not only was God still there, but in the dark night of sin, His face is still turned our way.

---

[4] Leslie Hardinge, *With Jesus in His Sanctuary* (Harrisburg, PA: American Cassette Ministries, 1991), p. 201.

[5] See Genesis 15:7 and Exodus 13:21 for examples.

[6] Hardinge, p. 204

[7] Hugh Martin, p. 35

[8] Jamieson, Fausset and Brown. *Jamieson Fausset Brown Bible Commentary,* 1871, comments on Genesis 3:24

C H A P T E R   T H R E E

The City of God

Nothing obstructs your view of the magnificent night sky during the depths of the Canadian winter. There comes a point when the mercury in the thermometer drops so low that cloud cover becomes impossible, and if you are lucky enough to get away from the bright lights of the big city, the view will leave you speechless. It will also leave you utterly reassured that our small blue planet is only an infinitesimally small part of the cosmos.

When Jean and I lived near the Alaska Highway, I would sometimes pull over to the side of the road late at night just to spend a few minutes looking up. Stepping out into less-than-minus-forty temperatures, I would wade my way through squeaky dry snow to a clearing above a river chasm where my view was completely unobstructed. And even though it was cold enough outside to end your life (if you were unfortunate enough to lose the protection of your winter gear and become exposed to the elements) I would still take a few minutes to lie down on the ground and watch the stars.

The silence of a cold winter's night almost makes the brilliance of the stars seem audible. I envy the ancients whose skies were consistently unpolluted by either smog or lights, because they were able to see—and hear—so much more than we do. Modern civilization has stolen something from us. Even when we do manage to venture outside of city limits at night, we ride in a vehicle with a roof on it, and the headlights keep our eyes from seeing the finest nuances of our cosmic neighborhood. We fail, most of the time, to notice a Presence that is eager to speak to our hearts.

— ❦ —

"Come outside with me, Abraham, I've got something to show you."

"What is it, Lord?"

"Just come outside and take a look."

Abraham stepped outside of his tent and followed God into the cool night air. They had just been talking about the future, and Abraham was having a little trouble believing what he had just been told. He was going to have a son—in spite of the fact that his wife was past her childbearing years. Of course he knew that the Creator had promised to make a great nation of his family, but up to this point there wasn't much indication that it was really going to happen. His only hope of becoming a great nation was to hand off his little empire to his servant, Eleazar—but that was not the same as having his own son.

"Don't worry," God told him in a vision. "You're going to have a son of your own, and your family will become a great nation of people who serve Me. Now come and take a look."

The night sky in Abraham's day was magnificent. Millions of sparkling stars that looked as if they might be close enough to touch hung over his head.

Then He brought him outside and said, "Look now toward heaven, and count the stars if you are able to number them." And He said to him, "So shall your descendants be." (Genesis 15:5)

The amazing thing about counting stars is that you never seem to be finished. As your eyes adjust to lower and lower levels of light, more and more stars reveal themselves. No matter how carefully you partition off sections of the sky for counting, you will always come back and find a few more stars that you hadn't noticed the first time you looked. God's promise to Abraham was staggering: your descendants will be so numerous that nobody will be able to count them all.

Looking down through time, the disciple John saw the fulfillment of God's promise to Abraham:

After these things I looked, and behold, a great multitude which no one could number, of all nations, tribes, peoples, and tongues, standing before the throne and before the Lamb, clothed with white robes, with palm branches in their hands, and crying out with a loud voice, saying, "Salvation belongs to our God who sits on the throne, and to the Lamb!" (Revelation 7:9, 10)

The group in heaven is made up from people of all nations. How can they all be Abraham's descendants? Grab a Bible and read the context carefully. This passage in Revelation is set in the context of the twelve tribes of Israel. Just before you read about a great crowd that nobody can number, John describes a mysterious last-day group of people known as the 144,000. In this group, there are 12,000 from each of the tribes of Israel. Immediately after the angel describes this group to John, he turns and sees a great crowd.

I won't spend much time on the 144,000, because it is not the subject of this book, but I would like to point out that the innumerable company of redeemed believers is at least *linked* to the descendants of Israel. It is not the *literal* nation of Israel, because they are from every tribe on earth. Rather, it is *spiritual* Israel. The book of Galatians informs us that God counts anyone who claims Christ as Savior as one of Abraham's descendants:

And if you are Christ's, then you are Abraham's seed, and heirs according to the promise. (Galatians 3:29)

Believers are Abraham's descendants. They are heirs to the promise that God made thousands of years ago. Their spiritual ancestor was a man faithful enough to leave his ancestral home and follow God in a new direction, and like him, they have also left the world to follow God.

Abraham pulled up his tent stakes and moved from Chaldea to Canaan, looking for a piece of real estate that God had promised him. And while he was moving to a literal piece of land, it wasn't really what God—or Abraham—ultimately had in mind:

By faith Abraham obeyed when he was called to go out to the place which he would receive as an inheritance. And he went out, not knowing where he was going. By faith he dwelt in the land of promise as in a foreign country, dwelling in tents with Isaac and Jacob, the heirs with him of the same promise; for he waited for the city which has foundations, whose builder and maker is God. (Hebrews 11:8-10)

The Bible says that Abraham was looking for a city that *God* built, and as far as I know, no such city existed in the region of Canaan at the time. So where was this city that Abraham was looking for? It is mentioned in the book of Revelation:

Then I, John, saw the holy city, New Jerusalem, coming down out of heaven from God, prepared as a bride adorned for her husband. And I heard a loud voice from heaven saying, "Behold, the tabernacle of God is with men, and He will dwell with them, and they shall be His people. God Himself will be with them and be their God." (Revelation 21:2, 3)

The city that God builds is the *new* Jerusalem, and it descends to planet earth after the Second Coming of Christ. When Abraham moved away from Ur, he understood that he was not only going to inherit the literal land of Canaan; he was also going to inherit the heavenly city. And there, he would dwell in the very presence of God.

If you take a good look at the covenant that God established with Abraham, you will discover that is what God had in mind, too. One of the most remarkable things about Abraham—this amazing man that at least three of the world's great religions claim as a spiritual hero and at least two of the world's ethnic groups claim as a direct genetic ancestor—is that God claimed him as a personal friend. No fewer than three times the Bible says that Abraham was the "friend of God."

Take, for example, this passage found in the book of 2 Chronicles, where Jehoshaphat, king of Israel, is praying to God. Notice what he says as he addresses the Almighty Creator of the universe:

"Are You not our God, who drove out the inhabitants of this land before Your people Israel, and gave it to the descendants of Abraham Your friend forever? And they dwell in it, and have built You a sanctuary in it for Your name..." (2 Chronicles 20:7, 8)

I want you to notice a few things in this verse. First of all, Jehoshaphat refers to the Creator as "our" God—as the God of Israel. There was a personal relationship between God and the descendants of Abraham. Secondly, the king mentions that once the Israelites had conquered the land of Canaan, they built a sanctuary so that the presence of God could dwell among them. And then, lastly, he mentions that Abraham was a "friend of God."

In many of the world's religions, God is described either as an impersonal force that anonymously directs the universe, or as an impatient dictator who gets angry if He doesn't get His way. In either case, it creates a situation in which devotees worship Him out of mere principle or out of a sense of fear. This was not the God that Abraham knew.

Abraham's God wants a *relationship* with people. In the Garden of Eden He enjoyed visiting with Adam in the cool of the evening. After sin, He established His Presence at the gates of the Garden as a constant reminder that He still wants to be with us. And then, as God established His covenant with Abraham, He called Abraham His *friend*—and He sealed the promise by showing up in Person.

In Genesis 15, where God promised Abraham that his descendants would be like the stars of heaven, the Bible describes a strange ritual:

Then He said to him, "I am the LORD, who brought you out of Ur of the Chaldeans, to give you this land to inherit it." And he said, "Lord GOD, how shall I know that I will inherit it?" So He said to him, "Bring Me a three-year-old heifer, a three-year-old female goat, a three-year-old ram, a turtledove, and a young pigeon." Then he brought all these to Him and cut them in two, down the middle, and placed each piece opposite the other; but he did not cut the birds in two. (Gen. 15:7-10)

Sacrifices were something that God's people had already been performing for generations. Every innocent animal that lost its life was a symbol pointing forward to the day when God's Son would give His own innocent life in order to pay the penalty for of our sins. Each sacrifice was like a pledge that, by faith, we accepted the death of God's Son in our behalf. We were placing our faith completely in what God could accomplish for us, because we knew we could not solve the sin problem ourselves. It is only natural that Abraham would offer a sacrifice when God was promising him both the land of Canaan and a heavenly inheritance. He knew that his inheritance was not earned; it was a gift from God that was made possible by the sacrifice of the coming Messiah.

Bible scholars have also noted that it was commonplace in the ancient world to establish a solemn covenant by sacrificing animals. In fact, it is quite possible that the modern expression "to cut a deal" might be left over from this ancient practice, and some have suggested that the reason an animal was sacrificed when a contract was established was to prove that the contract was final and unalterable. It was as permanent as death. That means that the covenant God established with Abraham was unalterable. When Christ died on the cross, the deal was sealed. God will never go back on His agreement with Abraham, and He will never revoke His end of the promise to save you for the Kingdom of Heaven.

There is finality—permanence—to the promises of God. Even though human beings may renege on their promises almost every day, God will never do so. We can rest in the fact that the covenant of salvation, the promise made to Abraham, will never be changed. One day, there will be a group of people standing in the Kingdom of Heaven so large that no one can number it, just as God promised. And because you can be Abraham's descendant through Christ, you can be numbered in that group.

When Abraham entered into a covenant with God, not only was there a sacrifice to seal it, God Himself did something unusual. He showed up in Person!

Years ago, when I was growing up in Canada, I remember a particularly clear winter night like the ones I described earlier. I was riding in a car with my father. Suddenly, a big black shape—about the size of a Volkswagen Beetle—silently flew across the sky right over our heads and disappeared into the hills on the horizon. It was outlined with dazzling blue fire, and long flames shot out behind it. A meteor! I doubt I will ever forget it.

Abraham saw something even more spectacular. The Bible says that a deep impenetrable darkness enveloped the night, and then Abraham witnessed the very presence of God:

Now when the sun was going down, a deep sleep fell upon Abram; and behold, horror and great darkness fell upon him...And it came to pass, when the sun went down and it was dark, that behold, there appeared a smoking oven and a burning torch that passed between those pieces. (Genesis 15:12, 17)

All through the Bible, fire is used as a symbol of God's presence. That night, as Abraham faced the darkness of discouragement, God drew close. He stepped into human history and revealed Himself. He has, after all, always wanted to *be with us*.

Some people think about God in all the wrong ways. I have met people who think God begrudgingly listens to our prayers because He has no choice but to listen. They think that He only lets people into the Kingdom of Heaven because He has no choice if we happened to earn enough points to get in. "All right," He sighs, "I guess you can come in. I don't really want you here, but what choice do I have?"

Nothing could be further from the truth. The book of Revelation says that we were originally created for God's pleasure. As He was creating the human race, a smile of delight must have spread across His face. He could see the great times that we would have together. We were designed for *joy*—both ours, and God's.

There is no question that our *sins* have angered and saddened God. But, remarkably, they haven't changed His desire to be with *us*. That is why, in the dark of the night, as the horrors of a rough future were pressing in on Abraham, God came in person. He revealed His presence. Sometimes when the night of our existence is the darkest, and the winter of our experience is the coldest, we will discover that the stars are shining at their absolute brightest.

CHAPTER FOUR

Living Fire

In the ancient world it was about the biggest demotion you could get. It was probably a good thing that Moses only had sheep for company, because that way he didn't have to explain his station in life to curious people at social gatherings. *Shepherd* was about the lowest position on the career totem pole, and with an education from the finest institutions of the most advanced civilization of the day, it must have been tempting for Moses—at least once in a while—to think that he was overqualified for the position.

He used to have it all—but then he threw it away. He did something stupid, and was forced to flee from Egypt. Now he watched a flock of sheep for his father-in-law. It was like getting demoted from four-star general down to a private with non-stop latrine duty.

Then, after 40 years of moving sheep from one field to the next, something utterly remarkable happened:

Now Moses was tending the flock of Jethro his father-in-law, the priest of Midian. And he led the flock to the back of the desert, and came to Horeb, the mountain of God. And the Angel of the LORD appeared to him in a flame of fire from the midst of a bush. So he looked, and behold, the bush was burning with fire, but the bush was not consumed. Then Moses said, "I will now turn aside and see this great sight, why the bush does not burn." (Exodus 3:1-3)

A bush in flames was not an uncommon occurrence. A bush in flames that *did not burn* was highly unusual! It was enough to make Moses step off the trail to investigate, and that's when he had a direct encounter with the Presence of God.

God didn't manifest Himself in the middle of the trail or stand directly in Moses' path. The Bible says that Moses had to "turn aside" to look at the burning bush, which teaches us something valuable about how God chooses to operate in our lives. He often waits for us to step outside of our usual routines to have an encounter with Him.

Sometimes we fail to notice God's presence because we have established a path in life that does not include Him. We fall out of bed in the morning, wolf down a hasty breakfast, dive into the car to fight for a place in the morning rush hour, put in somewhere between eight and fifteen hours at the office, watch a little TV in bed before falling asleep—only to start the whole process again the next morning.

Eventually you come to the point where you have spent your entire life eating, sleeping and working—and still complain that the presence of God was nowhere to be felt throughout most of your life. Moses had to *step off the trail* to encounter the presence of God. And as he ventured away from the ordinary routine of life, he made an amazing discovery: a bush on fire that didn't burn up. It was the strangest thing he had ever seen:

So when the LORD saw that he turned aside to look, God called to him from the midst of the bush and said, "Moses, Moses!" And he said, "Here I am." Then He said, "Do not draw near this place. Take your sandals off your feet, for the place where you stand is holy ground." Moreover He said, "I am the God of your father—the God of Abraham, the God of Isaac, and the God of Jacob." And Moses hid his face, for he was afraid to look upon God. (Exodus 3:4-6)

Notice how God established contact with Moses. First He did something to attract his attention. *Then He waited for a response.* The Bible says that "when the Lord saw that he turned aside to look," He called Moses by name.

I once met a young man who was raised as an atheist but was struggling with the overwhelming evidence he had seen for God's existence.

"Listen!" he said to me one evening. "How can I know for sure that

God is *really* there? For everything else in life I can do the math. I can collect the evidence and come to a rock-solid conclusion. But with this religion stuff, I can't seem to get any more evidence."

At this point, he actually had *plenty* of evidence.

"Mike," I said gently, "I'm afraid God's not likely to give you any more to go on until you take a few steps in His direction based on what you already have. He is not going to force Himself into your life, and you're going to have to give some indication that you really *want* a relationship with Him."

At some point in life, you have to take that first step off the path to go and investigate the burning bush. You are going to have to act on what you already know before you are going to see any more. You have to step off of the trail. When you do, God responds by calling your name.

"Moses! Moses!" Can't you hear the excitement in God's voice when he finally comes over to the burning bush? It's almost as if God is sitting on the edge of His seat, waiting for Moses to come.

Here is an important question: who was in that burning bush? Was it really just an angel, as verse two suggests? Not exactly. Adam Clarke, the famous Methodist preacher and commentator, made this fascinating observation:

Not a created angel certainly; for he is called Jehovah...*and has the most expressive attributes of the Godhead applied to him...Yet he is an* angel, malach, *a messenger, in whom was the name of God, chap. xxiii. 21; and in whom dwelt all the fullness of the Godhead bodily, Col. ii.9; and who, in all these primitive times, was the Messenger of the covenant, Mal iii.1.[9]*

If, as Mr. Clarke suggests, the Presence in the bush was not a created angel,[10] who was it? There is an important clue to this Being's identity in the way that He addresses Moses. He uses Moses' name *twice.*

Page through the Bible to see if you can find anybody else with this interesting character trait. I think you will notice an interesting pattern. In 1 Samuel 3, God calls Samuel in the middle of the night, and He uses his name twice: "Samuel! Samuel!"

Turn to the New Testament, and you find this same pattern:

And Jesus answered and said to her, "Martha, Martha, you are worried and troubled about many things." (Luke 10:41)

Then he fell to the ground, and heard a voice saying to him, "Saul,

Saul, why are you persecuting Me?" And he said, "Who are You, Lord?"
Then the Lord said, "I am Jesus, whom you are persecuting..."
(Acts 9:4-6)

I know it is not conclusive evidence, but it *is* interesting that Jesus was in the habit of using people's names twice! Was it *Jesus* in the burning bush?

The evidence of Scripture removes any doubt. When Moses asks the Presence who he should say had been speaking to him, God responds, "I AM THAT I AM."[11] In the gospel of John, when the religious leaders of Israel are voicing their personal doubts to Jesus, He indicates that He is the "I AM"—the One who appeared to Abraham and Moses.[12]

Jesus is the God of the Old Testament. Not only does the Bible clearly point out that Jesus is the Creator[13], it also points out that Jesus is the One who has maintained contact with us and manifested His presence among us ever since we fell into sin.

It is wonderful to discover that we can still experience the Presence of God. It's also a little frustrating, because there are limits on how close we can come:

Then He said, "Do not draw near this place. Take your sandals off your feet, for the place where you stand is holy ground." Moreover He said, "I am the God of your father—the God of Abraham, the God of Isaac, and the God of Jacob." And Moses hid his face, for he was afraid to look upon God. (Exodus 3:5, 6)

The fear of God's presence, first felt by Adam, was bequeathed to the entire sinful human race. Moses hid his face, because the presence of God made him afraid. While God's Presence can be both comforting and exhilarating for us, it is also a cause for concern, because we know that the sin in our hearts makes us unfit for the occasion. There is a clear example of these kinds of mixed emotions in the book of Isaiah, where the prophet is suddenly taken—in vision—into the throne room of God:

In the year that King Uzziah died, I saw the Lord sitting on a throne, high and lifted up, and the train of His robe filled the temple. Above it stood seraphim; each one had six wings: with two he covered his face, with two he covered his feet, and with two he flew. And one cried to another and said: "Holy, holy, holy is the LORD of hosts; the whole earth is full of His glory!" And the posts of the door were shaken by the voice of him who cried out, and the house was filled with smoke. Then I said: "Woe is me, for I am undone! Because I am a man of unclean lips, and I dwell in the midst of a people of unclean lips; for my eyes have seen the King, the LORD of hosts." (Isaiah 6:1-5)

Notice that on the one hand, Isaiah describes the amazing splendor of God's presence, but on the other, he feels an immediate sense of horrific unworthiness. Likewise, Moses is irresistibly drawn to the Presence of God, but as he draws closer, he becomes uncomfortable because he knows his sins make him utterly unworthy.

The problem of sin is like the glass barrier that exists between an incarcerated husband and his visiting wife. It puts a limit on how close we can come to God. We are like a poor street kid looking through a bakery window at all of the wonderful things we can never have.

If God was going to restore us to His Presence, He was going to have to make some special arrangements.

---

[9] Adam Clarke's commentary on Exodus 3:2
[10] The word "angel" is sometimes used to describe angelic beings; other times it is simply used to describe a messenger, since that is the literal meaning of the word.
[11] Exodus 3:14
[12] John 8:58
[13] John 1:1-3; Colossians 1:16, 17; and Hebrews 1:1, 2

CHAPTER FIVE

Blueprints of Heaven

The Sears Company used to sell housing kits. These were different than modern prefabricated homes; they were actual housing kits that came with everything you needed to assemble the home of your dreams yourself—and it came with as many as 30,000 pieces! According to one CBS news story, the housing kit came with "750 pounds of nails, 27 gallons of paint and varnish, 10 pounds of wood putty, 460 pounds of window weight, 27 windows, 25 doors and a 75-page instruction book."[14] Sears and Roebuck claimed that a "man of average ability" would be able to put it all together in about 90 days.

Between the years of 1908 and 1940 Sears sold more than 100,000 mail-order buildings, including houses, apartment buildings and even barns. The homes were wildly popular for a while, because they were inexpensive and easy to assemble. By following the instruction manual and doing all the labor yourself, you might just save yourself between $500 and $2000—which was a fortune at the beginning of last century. These savings have been referred to as "sweat equity," because you had to work hard for it.

The Sears company was not the first to come up with the idea; other companies had done it before them. But thousands of years before any company came up with the idea, God did something similar with the Israelites. He gave them detailed instructions and told them exactly which materials to build with as they constructed a tabernacle to house His Presence.

God had made a solemn covenant with Abraham that He would lead his descendants out of Egyptian slavery back into the Promised Land. And when the time came for the fulfillment of the promise, God took it upon Himself to personally lead the Israelites across the desert:

And the LORD went before them by day in a pillar of cloud to lead the way, and by night in a pillar of fire to give them light, so as to go by day and night. He did not take away the pillar of cloud by day or the pillar of fire by night from before the people. (Exodus 13:21, 22)

The Apostle Paul reveals which member of the Godhead was leading Israel in that pillar of fire and cloud. Speaking of the Presence of God as it guided them across the desert, Paul says of the Israelites that:

...they drank of that spiritual Rock that followed them, and that Rock was Christ. (1 Corinthians 10:4b)

It was the pre-incarnate Christ who appeared to Moses in the burning bush, and it was the pre-incarnate Christ who led the Israelites across the desert into the land of Canaan. He was with His people, traveling in a pillar of fire by night, and a pillar of cloud by day. But He wasn't content to simply be *near* His people; He wanted to be *with* them. And that is how the first "housing kit" came into existence. Speaking to Moses, God asked for something very special:

"And let them make Me a sanctuary, that I may dwell among them. According to all that I show you, that is, the pattern of the tabernacle and the pattern of all its furnishings, just so you shall make it."
(Exodus 25:8, 9)

When Moses built the sanctuary that God requested, he wasn't allowed to get creative. God instructed him to follow a very specific blueprint. Not only would the tabernacle house the presence of God—the *Shekinah*—every time the Israelites pitched camp; it was also a vivid object lesson that detailed God's plans to restore His people to full communion with Him. By examining the sanctuary, the children of Israel (and the whole world, for that matter) could study God's detailed plan to bring them back into full communion with Him.

The book of Psalms says, "Your way, O God, is in the sanctuary" (Psalm 77:13a). Nothing in the tabernacle was designed for purely esthetic purposes; it was all done deliberately. It allowed the presence of God to dwell among the Israelites without consuming them, and it allowed the Israelites to draw closer to Him by learning about Him through the rituals of the tabernacle.

The wilderness sanctuary had three basic sections: an *outer courtyard* surrounded by a high fence, where animal sacrifices took place on a daily basis; the *Holy Place*, into which the priests carried the blood of sacrificial animals every day; and the *Most Holy Place*, the innermost chamber where the presence of God would literally take up residence above the Ark of the Covenant.

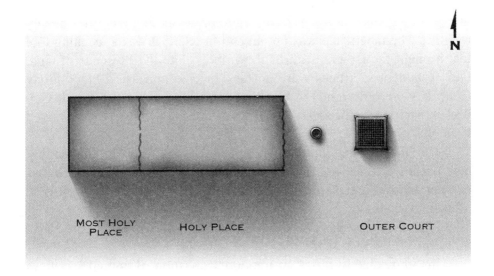

MOST HOLY PLACE   HOLY PLACE   OUTER COURT

What was the blueprint used to build this structure? The book of Hebrews gives us an important clue. Speaking of Jesus, it says:

Now this is the main point of the things we are saying: We have such a High Priest, who is seated at the right hand of the throne of the Majesty in the heavens, a Minister of the sanctuary and of the true tabernacle which the Lord erected, and not man. (Hebrews 8:1, 2)

If you are not paying careful attention, it is easy to skip over a very important detail in this passage. Jesus is "a minister" of a "true tabernacle" that was set up by God Himself. The tabernacle in the wilderness was clearly built by human hands. Does this mean it was not the "true" tabernacle? A few verses later, speaking of the priests who worked in Moses' sanctuary, the Bible says they:

...serve the copy and shadow of the heavenly things, as Moses was divinely instructed when he was about to make the tabernacle. For He said, "See that you make all things according to the pattern shown you on the mountain." (Hebrews 8:5)

The author of Hebrews makes it clear that the Old Testament tabernacle, along with its rituals and priests, were *copies* of a greater reality in heaven. And it is that greater reality that served as the blueprint Moses used to build the earthly tabernacle. It was a copy of the sanctuary in *heaven*—one that God Himself built.

The fact that the earthly tabernacle was a mere shadow of the one in heaven tells us that it was designed to draw our attention to heavenly realities. The tabernacle was not an end in itself; it was a teaching tool that brought the Israelites, through symbols, into the Presence of God. Old Testament sacrifices were not designed to appease a bloodthirsty God; they were designed to teach us something about the length God was prepared to go through in order to restore everything we have ruined through sin.

Even though the animals sacrificed on the altar in the earthly tabernacle were clearly offered as penance for sin, the book of Hebrews is clear that animal sacrifices themselves were actually powerless to offer forgiveness to anyone:

For it is not possible that the blood of bulls and goats could take away sins. (Hebrews 10:4)

This immediately raises an important question: if animal sacrifices couldn't provide forgiveness for sins, why offer them at all? It's really quite simple. Each animal offered on the altar was a symbol of faith. The ancient Israelites were anticipating the arrival of a Messiah who would offer His own life as a sacrifice for their sins. As each lamb was offered, the Israelites would place their hands on its head and confess their sins. The sins were thus symbolically transferred to the sacrificial animal, and the person offering the lamb would take its life. This reminded the one offering the sacrifice that the results of his sins were horrible.

I have often tried to imagine the pain of taking an innocent lamb's life, knowing that it would die because *I* had sinned. Sin isn't trivial. It leads to death.[15] Every lamb that was sacrificed became a painful reminder of how serious the consequences of sin really are. If it was a matter of putting food on the table, you might be able to reassure yourself that you were killing the lamb for a good reason. But in the sacrificial service, the *only* reason for the lamb's death was your sin.

The lamb was a powerful symbol pointing forward to the day that the Messiah would take our sins upon Himself—and it was the faith of the penitent sinner in the coming Messiah that secured his forgiveness, not the animal itself.

Throughout the Bible, Jesus is referred to over and over again as a *lamb*. In fact, it happens nearly 30 times in the book of Revelation alone, a clear indication that all of the sacrificial lambs of the Old Testament sanctuary pointed to Him. Seeing Jesus for the first time, John the Baptist said, "Behold, the Lamb of God, which takes away the sins of the world" (John 1:29). The prophet Isaiah, predicting what Christ would do for us at the cross, said, "He was led as a lamb to the slaughter" (Isaiah 53:7).

If the sins of Old Testament believers were symbolically transferred to an innocent lamb before it was sacrificed, then we can conclude that our sins are transferred to Jesus when we confess them. That is why Paul said, in 2 Corinthians 5:21, that Jesus was "made to be sin for us." As He hung on Calvary's cross, He was volunteering Himself to be the sacrificial lamb for the sins of the world. He took your place and paid for your transgressions.

It has become popular in some streams of modern Christianity to suggest that salvation is free—that it doesn't cost anything. That is simply not true. You will never be able to buy your salvation, and there is nothing you can do to earn it, but it still cost the Son of God everything He had. If people spent a thoughtful hour reflecting on the cross of Christ each day, they would quickly stop trivializing sin and put it in its proper perspective.

Once the lamb was slain, its blood was carried into the first compartment of the sanctuary, which was called the *Holy Place*. There a priest would sprinkle the blood against the veil that separated the Holy Place from the Most Holy Place—the innermost compartment of the sanctuary where the Ark of the Covenant was kept. As the priest sprinkled the blood against the veil he was presenting it before the Presence of God, a vivid picture of Jesus presenting His own blood before the throne of heaven as atonement for our sins:

Therefore, brethren, having boldness to enter the Holiest by the blood of Jesus, by a new and living way which He consecrated for us, through the veil, that is, His flesh, and having a High Priest over the house of God, let us draw near with a true heart in full assurance of faith, having our hearts sprinkled from an evil conscience and our bodies washed with pure water. (Hebrews 10:19-22)

And according to the law almost all things are purified with blood, and without shedding of blood there is no remission. Therefore it was necessary that the copies of the things in the heavens should be purified with these, but the heavenly things themselves with better sacrifices than these. For Christ has not entered the holy places made with hands, which are copies of the true, but into heaven itself, now to appear in the presence of God for us. (Hebrews 9:22-24)

The reason that God wanted Moses to build the sanctuary was simple: He wanted His people to catch a glimpse of what was going on behind the scenes to save them. He wanted them to become intimately acquainted with His plans for them. In establishing the tabernacle and its services, He brought a little piece of heaven down to earth. It was a replica of the sanctuary in heaven. Then He took up residence in the camp of Israel, sending a clear signal that His greatest desire was to live among His people and restore access to His throne.

The book of Hebrews reassures us that today we can step boldly into the presence of God, even though we are sinners. Jesus has paved the way. He is both the sacrificial lamb *and* heaven's great High Priest. His innocent blood, which He shed as a member of our human race, has made it possible for you to come closer to the Presence of God. And why would Jesus be interested in making that possible? It's because *your* presence is what He craves most.

---

[14] CBS News Sunday Morning, *The Mail-Order House*, August 24, 2003
[15] Romans 6:23

CHAPTER SIX

Into the Sanctuary

The famous artist Holman Hunt once told his friends that he was planning to paint a picture of Jesus Christ. His friends protested, insisting that such a task was utterly impossible. "A real artist can only paint something he can see," they said, "so obviously you can't paint Jesus, because you've never seen Him!"

"But you don't understand," Hunt said. "I *am* going to see Him. I will work by His side in the carpenter's shop. I will walk with Him over the hills of Galilee. I will go with Him among the poor, the blind, the naked, the lepers. I will travel with Him to Calvary and climb the cross with Him, until I see Him and know Him, and then I will paint Him."

Holman Hunt found a way to see Jesus when Jesus wasn't physically present: by studying His life in the words of the Bible. Today millions continue to find Him through the words that His disciples wrote down for us. But what would you do if you lived thousands of years before the gospels were written? How would you find Jesus then? The Bible makes it clear that, as the Creator, Jesus' existence did not begin when He was born as a human in Bethlehem. He has existed from "everlasting."

"But you, Bethlehem Ephrathah, though you are little among the thousands of Judah, yet out of you shall come forth to Me the One to be Ruler in Israel, whose goings forth are from of old, From everlasting." *(Micah 5:2)*

In the last chapter, we discovered that Jesus accompanied the Israelites across the desert, and made direct contact with people on occasion, as He did with Moses at the burning bush. There are a number of other examples in the Old Testament where Christ appears to Old Testament believers, including a mysterious encounter experienced by Moses' successor, Joshua:

And it came to pass, when Joshua was by Jericho, that he lifted his eyes and looked, and behold, a Man stood opposite him with His sword drawn in His hand. And Joshua went to Him and said to Him, "Are You for us or for our adversaries?" So He said, "No, but as Commander of the army of the LORD I have now come." And Joshua fell on his face to the earth and worshiped, and said to Him, "What does my Lord say to His servant?" Then the Commander of the LORD's army said to Joshua, "Take your sandal off your foot, for the place where you stand is holy." And Joshua did so. (Joshua 5:13-15)

Why do Bible scholars identify this passage as an encounter with the pre-incarnate Christ? Look at it carefully. In Exodus 3:5, when Moses encountered the burning bush, he was told to take off his sandals because he was standing on holy ground, in the presence of God. Joshua is now told to do the same thing.

This mysterious Being—described as the "Commander of the Lord's army"—cannot be a mere angel, because Joshua bows down to worship Him. If this had been an angel, Joshua would have been told to rise to his feet and quit worshiping. (We know this because of the angel's response to John's adoration in Revelation 19:10.) Angels of God do not accept worship, but the "Commander of the Lord's army" *does*. And why is He called "the Commander of the Lord's army?" A stunning description of the Second Coming of Christ found in Revelation 19 makes it obvious:

Now I saw heaven opened, and behold, a white horse. And He who sat on him was called Faithful and True, and in righteousness He judges and makes war. His eyes were like a flame of fire, and on His head were many crowns. He had a name written that no one knew except Himself. He was clothed with a robe dipped in blood, and His name is called The Word of God. And the armies in heaven, clothed in fine linen, white and clean, followed Him on white horses. (Revelation 19:11-14)

On occasion, Jesus made personal appearances in the Old Testament. Outside of these personal appearances, however, there is no clearer picture of Him than the one found in the sanctuary, its furniture and its rituals. They were instituted as rituals of faith for Old Testament believers who were looking forward to Christ's arrival as the Messiah.

This means, of course, that Old Testament believers were forgiven and saved the same way it happens for believers today—through faith in Christ. There is a popular teaching in circulation that suggests that Old Testament believers were saved through obedience, but New Testament believers are saved by grace through faith. This simply isn't true. The Bible demonstrates—quite clearly—that the method of salvation for the sinner has always been the same.

The fourth chapter of Paul's letter to the Romans makes this abundantly clear:

What then shall we say that Abraham our father has found according to the flesh? For if Abraham was justified by works, he has something to boast about, but not before God. For what does the Scripture say? "Abraham believed God, and it was accounted to him for righteousness." Now to him who works, the wages are not counted as grace but as debt. But to him who does not work but believes on Him who justifies the ungodly, his faith is accounted for righteousness, just as David also describes the blessedness of the man to whom God imputes righteousness apart from works: "Blessed are those whose lawless deeds are forgiven, And whose sins are covered; Blessed is the man to whom the LORD shall not impute sin." (Romans 4:1-8)

Paul gives two Old Testament examples of salvation by faith through grace. Abraham did not *earn* his salvation; it was given to him as a gift because of his belief in God. (His belief was "accounted to him for righteousness.") David did not teach salvation through mere obedience; he taught that our sins are forgiven and covered, rather than paid off by personal effort. The message is clear: salvation has always been a gift obtained through faith in Christ.

Martin Luther is widely recognized as having rediscovered the principle of "righteousness by faith" during the early part of the sixteenth century, during a time when many people were trying to gain God's favor through acts of penance. As he attempted to earn forgiveness for sins by crawling up Pilate's Staircase in Rome, a passage from Romans suddenly leapt to mind: *the just shall live by faith* (Romans 1:17). It signaled a new day for Luther. He had studied the passage many times before, but now it became crystal clear. You simply cannot earn your salvation; you must accept by faith that Christ has dealt with the problem for you and then respond to His gift in love.

What many people fail to notice is that the principle Luther rediscovered is *not* a New Testament principle. The passage that revolutionized his thinking was actually a quote from the Old Testament book of Habakkuk:

"Behold the proud, his soul is not upright in him; but the just shall live by his faith." (Habakkuk 2:4)

Salvation through faith is an *Old Testament concept.* Nobody has ever earned salvation. Period. The eleventh chapter of Hebrews lists those honored for their faith, and not one person mentioned there is a New Testament believer. It was their *faith* that earned them a spot in God's "hall of fame," not their accomplishments:

But without faith it is impossible to please Him, for he who comes to God must believe that He is, and that He is a rewarder of those who diligently seek Him. (Hebrews 11:6)

Modern Christians look back to what Christ accomplished at the cross of Calvary, and through faith, they accept that His sacrifice was sufficient to pay their debt of sin and purchase their salvation. Old Testament believers were also "Christians" before the name was coined in the city of Antioch many years later.[16] They looked forward to what Christ would accomplish at the cross in the future. Their animal sacrifices were an act of faith; they demonstrated that they believed Christ's sacrifice would be sufficient to pay their debt of sin and purchase their salvation.

The Old Testament "church" looked forward to Christ's arrival through the ceremonies and rituals that took place in the tabernacle. They followed His Presence across the desert, they worshiped Him in the sanctuary, and they offered sacrifices as a symbol of faith in what He would accomplish for them. It was an entirely faith-based religion that rested completely on God's grace to accomplish salvation for them.

Hundreds of years before Jesus was born, and long before the gospels were written, the Israelites already had a clear picture of Him. The earthly tabernacle gave them a vivid portrayal of what the Messiah would accomplish for humanity.

The tabernacle essentially had three areas: an outer courtyard surrounded by a fence, the Holy Place and the Most Holy Place.

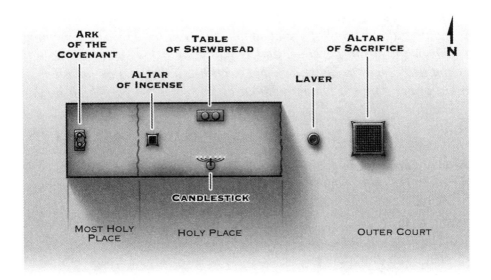

The Courtyard

Animals were sacrificed in the outer courtyard and offered on the Altar of Burnt Offering (or Altar of Sacrifice). Each animal sacrificed was a symbol of the Messiah, who would lay down His life for the sins of the world. The book of Hebrews makes this very clear:

Not with the blood of goats and calves, but with His own blood He entered the Most Holy Place once for all, having obtained eternal redemption. For if the blood of bulls and goats and the ashes of a heifer, sprinkling the unclean, sanctifies for the purifying of the flesh, how much more shall the blood of Christ, who through the eternal Spirit offered Himself without spot to God, cleanse your conscience from dead works to serve the living God? And for this reason He is the Mediator of the new covenant, by means of death, for the redemption of the transgressions under the first covenant, that those who are called may receive the promise of the eternal inheritance. (Hebrews 9:12-15)

Let's unpack that passage a little bit. It tells us that Jesus' blood replaced the "blood of goats and calves" and that His death took care of "transgressions under the first covenant." In other words, the animals were only symbolic; they did not save sinners. The blood of Christ saved them.

Here is an example of how the ritual of the "sin offering" took place in the Old Testament sanctuary:

If anyone of the common people sins unintentionally by doing
something against any of the commandments of the LORD in anything
which ought not to be done, and is guilty, or if his sin which he has
committed comes to his knowledge, then he shall bring as his offering
a kid of the goats, a female without blemish, for his sin which he has
committed. And he shall lay his hand on the head of the sin offering, and
kill the sin offering at the place of the burnt offering. Then the priest
shall take some of its blood with his finger, put it on the horns of the
altar of burnt offering, and pour all the remaining blood at the base of
the altar. He shall remove all its fat, as fat is removed from the sacrifice
of the peace offering; and the priest shall burn it on the altar for a sweet
aroma to the LORD. So the priest shall make atonement for him, and it
shall be forgiven him. (Leviticus 4:27-31)

This is an important passage to understand. The sacrificial victim had
to be an animal "without blemish," because Jesus is sinless.[17] The penitent
sinner laid his hands on the head of the sacrificial victim to confess his
sins and then killed the animal himself. This underscored the fact that the
lamb was dying for the person who brought it into the courtyard. There
was nobody else who could be held accountable for the lamb's death but
the one who cut its throat. Then the sacrificial animal was offered on the
Altar of Burnt offering. Through this ritual, *atonement* was made for the
sinner, and his sins were forgiven. He was considered clean and forgiven
before the throne of God.

The Altar of Burnt Offering points us directly to the cross of Christ,
where our sins were placed on God's Son. Looking forward to the day
that God's Sacrificial Lamb would give His life for us, the prophet Isaiah
described what happened in one of the most moving passages ever
written:

But He was wounded for our transgressions, He was bruised for
our iniquities; the chastisement for our peace was upon Him, and by
His stripes we are healed. All we like sheep have gone astray; we have
turned, every one, to his own way; and the LORD has laid on Him the
iniquity of us all. He was oppressed and He was afflicted, yet He opened
not His mouth; He was led as a lamb to the slaughter, and as a sheep
before its shearers is silent, so He opened not His mouth.
(Isaiah 53:5-7)

At the cross of Calvary, our sins were placed on Jesus. We deserve to die for them, but the innocent Jesus took them on Himself so that we can inherit the Kingdom of Heaven:

For He made Him who knew no sin to be sin for us, that we might become the righteousness of God in Him. (2 Corinthians 5:21)

...knowing that you were not redeemed with corruptible things, like silver or gold, from your aimless conduct received by tradition from your fathers, but with the precious blood of Christ, as of a lamb without blemish and without spot. (1 Peter 1:18, 19)

There is a remarkable exchange that took place at the cross. Our guilt was placed on God's perfect lamb, and Christ's perfect righteousness was given to us as a gift. One of my favorite Christian writers said it this way:

Christ was treated as we deserve, that we might be treated as He deserves. He was condemned for our sins, in which He had no share, that we might be justified by His righteousness, in which we had no share. He suffered the death which was ours, that we might receive the life which was His. "With His stripes we are healed."[18]

The next item found in the courtyard was a large copper basin containing water, situated between the Altar of Burnt Offering and the door to the tabernacle. This basin is commonly known as the *laver*. Any time a priest either approached the altar or took the blood of sacrificial victims inside the tabernacle, he had to wash his hands and feet with the water from the basin. Like the modern rite of Christian baptism, it was symbolic of the cleansing from sin that Christ offers us. Nobody could enter God's tabernacle—the place of His Presence—without first being cleansed from sin.

There is a passage in Paul's first letter to the Corinthian church that gives a shocking description of the sins of those who were members of the church:

Do you not know that the unrighteous will not inherit the kingdom of God? Do not be deceived. Neither fornicators, nor idolaters, nor adulterers, nor homosexuals, nor sodomites, nor thieves, nor covetous, nor drunkards, nor revilers, nor extortioners will inherit the kingdom of God. (1 Corinthians 6:9, 10)

If you're honest, you are going to find yourself mentioned in that list somewhere. Each of these sins is a violation of God's Ten Commandments, which were kept in the Most Holy Place. Committing any or all of these sins immediately disqualifies you from the kingdom of God and cuts you off from His presence. Through the gift of Christ, however, we can be forgiven, and our record is "washed" of any trace of sin. Listen to what Paul says next:

And such were some of you. But you were washed, but you were sanctified, but you were justified in the name of the Lord Jesus and by the Spirit of our God. (1 Corinthians 6:11)

The laver of the Old Testament sanctuary carried an important message. As we are, we are unfit to step into the presence of God, but Jesus makes it possible to become clean. You can be "washed" and "sanctified" (set aside for a holy purpose). In order to become clean and step into God's presence, you need to be washed by Jesus Christ.

The Holy Place

The tabernacle itself was divided into two rooms: the Holy Place and the Most Holy Place, separated by a thick embroidered veil. The Holy Place was the outer room where the priests worked every day. This is where they carried the blood of sacrificial animals. It had three articles of furniture: a seven-branched golden candlestick, a table for the "shewbread," and an altar for burned incense.

Each of these objects was designed to teach God's people something important about the Messiah. They were object lessons in the character of God, whose Presence was manifested in the Most Holy Place, just on the other side of the veil.

When the priest first walked into the Holy Place, there was a large *golden candlestick* immediately to his left. It stood almost five feet high and its branches, holding seven candles, spread out nearly three and a half feet.[19] This candlestick was made entirely of pure beaten gold, and weighed almost 200 pounds. It was the only source of light inside the sanctuary. On top of each branch was a small oil lamp, and it was the responsibility of the priests to keep them lit at all times.

This source of light was a powerful symbol of the Messiah. In a dramatic vision, the prophet Zechariah gives us some important clues to help us understand what God was trying to teach us through the candlestick. Zechariah was shown a candlestick being continuously supplied with olive oil to keep it burning. He asked the angel what it meant, and this is what he was told:

"This is the word of the LORD to Zerubbabel: 'Not by might nor by power, but by My Spirit,' Says the LORD of hosts." (Zechariah 4:6b)

The olive oil that filled the seven lamps was symbolic of the power of the Holy Spirit, the third Person of the Godhead. When Jesus began His public ministry at His baptism in the Jordan River, the Bible tells us that the Holy Spirit fell on Him, and a voice from heaven declared Him to be God's Son. At that moment, He began His Messianic ministry. He was a light that came to a world steeped in years of sin and darkness. John's gospel opens with a vivid description of Jesus as the "light" that came into a dark world,[20] and later in the same account, Jesus is recorded as saying:

"I am the light of the world. He who follows Me shall not walk in darkness, but have the light of life." (John 8:12)

The candlestick represents Jesus Christ, the light of the world. When He came to this world after thousands of years of spiritual darkness, it was as if someone had suddenly thrown on the lights in a dark room. Fallen angels had been lying to people about God's character for years, but now people could see for themselves—by watching Jesus—what God was really like.

This is underscored in a discussion that Philip had with Jesus:

Philip said to Him, "Lord, show us the Father, and it is sufficient for us." Jesus said to him, "Have I been with you so long, and yet you have not known Me, Philip? He who has seen Me has seen the Father; so how can you say, 'Show us the Father?' Do you not believe that I am in the Father, and the Father in Me? The words that I speak to you I do not speak on My own authority; but the Father who dwells in Me does the works." (John 14:8-10)

Jesus revealed the Father to us. Near the end of His time on earth, Jesus summed up His ministry among the disciples like this:

"O righteous Father! The world has not known You, but I have known You; and these have known that You sent Me. And I have declared to them Your name, and will declare it, that the love with which You loved Me may be in them, and I in them." (John 17:25, 26)

I have talked with many people who draw a sharp distinction between God the Father and God the Son. Some people say that the Father is an Old Testament figure, a "God of war," but the Son is a "God of love." The lessons of the sanctuary completely dispel this notion on two counts.

First of all, Jesus *is* the God of the Old Testament, and secondly, His ministry sheds a lot of light on the loving character of the Father.

Some people paint a horrible picture of God because they don't understand this. They suggest that Jesus continually has to run interference between sinners and the Father, because God the Father is eager to destroy sinners, but Jesus somehow manages to talk Him out of it. Nothing could be further from the truth, and the light of Christ's ministry proves it. Not only did He teach us that we could see the character of the Father in His life, but He also reminded us that the "Father Himself loves you."[21]

John also points out that "...God so loved the world that He gave His only begotten Son, that whoever believes in Him should not perish but have everlasting life" (John 3:16). It was the Father who gave His Son to the world—out of love!

The plan of salvation is not something that the Son cooked up simply to appease the Father. It was a plan developed by all three members of the Godhead out of love for the fallen human race. The ministry of Jesus proves it. When people spent time with Jesus, their hearts were opened, and many of them could see the light of truth for the very first time. They could sense, as they listened to His words, that God really *is* love. And when Jesus went to the cross, they knew it for sure.

Did the light go out when Jesus returned to heaven? Absolutely not. We still have access to it in the pages of the Bible and through the influence of the Holy Spirit, who is the heavenly oil that fuels the light. Years after Jesus ascended into heaven, the apostle John saw him in vision, dressed in sanctuary garments and standing in the midst of seven candlesticks:

Then I turned to see the voice that spoke with me. And having turned I saw seven golden lampstands, and in the midst of the seven lampstands One like the Son of Man, clothed with a garment down to the feet and girded about the chest with a golden band. (Revelation 1:12, 13)

What did this vision mean? The seven candles represent seven churches,[22] which in turn portray seven periods of church history between the ascension of Christ and His return. Christ's promise, in Hebrews 13: 5, is that He will never leave us or forsake us—and no matter what has happened over the centuries since He returned to heaven, Jesus has always been there with us. The light of the gospel will never be extinguished. Furthermore, the warm flames of the Holy Spirit were left behind to keep our eyes focused on Jesus:

"However, when He, the Spirit of truth, has come, He will guide you into all truth; for He will not speak on His own authority, but whatever He hears He will speak; and He will tell you things to come. He will glorify Me, for He will take of what is Mine and declare it to you." (John 16:13, 14)

Through the presence of the Holy Spirit, Jesus continues to fan the flames of the gospel in our hearts, and He asks us to carry that light to the whole world:

"Let your light so shine before men, that they may see your good works and glorify your Father in heaven." (Matthew 5:16)

The world should be able to see the light of Christ in our actions. The things we say and do should show the world what God is really like.

In addition to its light, the candlestick teaches us something else important about Jesus. It was made of a single slab of pure gold, beaten into shape by a master craftsman. As the hammer fell on the gold, blow after blow, the echoes spoke of another Light who would be beaten—for the sins of the human race. Remember the words of Isaiah?

Surely He has borne our griefs and carried our sorrows; yet we esteemed Him stricken, smitten by God, and afflicted. But He was wounded for our transgressions, He was bruised for our iniquities; the chastisement for our peace was upon Him, and by His stripes we are healed. (Isaiah 53:4, 5)

The Light that came into the world did not come easily or cheaply. Jesus had to endure unspeakable cruelties and live an unbearably hard life. He was crushed under the weight of our sins as he wrestled for our salvation in the Garden of Gethsemane. Great drops of blood fell from His forehead as He agonized over our salvation. The blows of Roman soldiers fell on His back as He was mercilessly beaten with a crude leather whip embedded with bits of steel. Worse than that, the blows of our sin fell on Him, and He ultimately poured out His life on the cross for us. Jesus endured the hammer of affliction until He bought our salvation—at the highest possible price. And thus, as a lesson for us, the candlestick was made from a single slab of beaten gold.

Across the room from the candlestick, on the right, was the *Table of Shewbread*. It was a wooden table overlaid with gold, a little more than two feet high and three feet long. There were 12 loaves of bread on top of the table, one loaf for each tribe in Israel. Like the candlestick, this bread also pointed to Jesus, who referred to Himself as the Bread of Life:

And Jesus said to them, "I am the bread of life. He who comes to Me shall never hunger, and he who believes in Me shall never thirst...I am the living bread which came down from heaven. If anyone eats of this bread, he will live forever; and the bread that I shall give is My flesh, which I shall give for the life of the world." (John 6:35, 51)

Bread is a symbol of Christ's body, which was given at the cross for our sins. When He chose this symbol, He chose something that everybody can relate to. Virtually every culture on earth has bread of some sort; it is a universal staple. And bread is not just important, it is indispensable—the same way that the sacrifice of Christ on the cross is not merely important; it is indispensable for our survival. Without His sacrifice, we would be completely lost in our sins.

Bread is a symbol of essential nutrition, and some of our everyday expressions underscore how important it is. When people gather for a meal, we sometimes say that they "broke bread together." The English word "companion" actually comes from two Latin words that mean "bread" and "together," so a "companion" is literally someone you share bread with. Someone who works for a living is called a "breadwinner," because bread is such a basic necessity of life. During the last century, "bread" even became slang for "money," because you simply can't live without it. Bread is an essential component of human survival.

When Jesus compared His body to bread, He was trying to tell us that we need Him *desperately*. The cross was not a frivolous extra. It was not icing on a cake or a decorative garnish on His ministry. Without the cross, mankind could have no union with the Father. There would be no salvation, just as without bread, entire civilizations starve to death. Christ's sacrifice is the source of our eternal life.

Every week, when the priests replaced the bread in the sanctuary, they encountered a vivid reminder that our very lives depend on the presence of the Creator. He is a staple that we can't live without.

There was a third article of furniture in the Holy Place, right up against the veil, at the far end of the room: the *Altar of Burned Incense.* It was much smaller than the Altar of Burnt Sacrifice in the courtyard, only about three feet high and two and a quarter feet square. The High

Priest burned a special compound of spices on this golden altar. If anyone tried to duplicate this special incense for any other purpose, he was immediately and permanently evicted from the camp of Israel. And the only fire that could be used to burn the incense had to come from the Altar of Sacrifice. It produced a sweet-smelling smoke that rose up from the altar and went over the veil into the Most Holy Place—into the Presence of God.

What was the meaning of this altar with its sweet-smelling smoke? Remember: everything in the earthly sanctuary was a copy of something in heaven. In the book of Revelation, we are given a remarkable glimpse into the meaning of this altar as John is shown the one located in heaven:

Then another angel, having a golden censer, came and stood at the altar. He was given much incense, that he should offer it with the prayers of all the saints upon the golden altar which was before the throne. And the smoke of the incense, with the prayers of the saints, ascended before God from the angel's hand. (Revelation 8:3, 4)

The smoke of the altar represents our prayers ascending into God's Presence. Our lives are so tainted by sin, however, that our prayers are also corrupted by selfishness, and on their own, they will never be worthy of appearing before God's throne. Jesus mixes our prayers with heavenly incense, the sweet fragrant offering of His perfect life, to make them acceptable. He blends them with His own righteousness to make them smell sweet in the courts of heaven.

As we stammer out our imperfect prayers, which are compromised by our selfishness and sin, Jesus mingles them with His own prayers, purifying them. The priests were forbidden to use any fire except the flames from the Altar of Sacrifice, because the only thing that makes us acceptable before the judgment seat of God is the sacrifice of Jesus at the cross.

The Old Testament sanctuary and its services created a number of valuable opportunities for God's people. It gave them a vivid picture of God's plan to save them and restore them to His presence. It also made it easy to recognize the Messiah when He came. The whole tabernacle—every bit of it—pointed to something that Jesus would do for His people. And today, if you study it carefully, you will still discover remarkable things about a God whose greatest desire is to be with His people.

The story is told of a Baptist pastor by the name of Peter Miller who lived in the state of Pennsylvania. Michael Wittman also lived in that town, a godless man who took great delight in embarrassing and humiliating preachers. On more than one occasion, Pastor Miller became his special target. He never missed an opportunity to publicly humiliate this man of God.

Eventually, Michael Wittman's misguided lifestyle caught up with him. He was arrested for treason and sentenced to die. When Pastor Miller heard about Michael's fate, he traveled 70 miles—on foot—to see General George Washington and plead for the traitor's life.

General Washington listened very carefully to Peter Miller's story, but when the kindly pastor was finished, he refused to save Michael Wittman. "I'm sorry," he said, "but I simply can't grant you the life of your friend."

"My friend!" Peter exclaimed. "Why, he's the worst enemy I have!"

Washington was surprised. "Do you mean to tell me that you traveled 70 miles on foot to save the life of your worst enemy? I've never heard of anything like it! That puts the whole matter in a different light. I'm going to grant him the pardon he doesn't deserve."

Michael Wittman was released, and he traveled home with Pastor Miller. To the day they died, they were the closest of friends.

What does the sanctuary teach us about God? He longs to place His Presence among us, and He was willing to travel an impossible road to make it happen. We declared ourselves to be God's enemy. He was willing to die on the Altar of Sacrifice so that we could step into the Most Holy Place—into His presence.

---

[16] Acts 11:26. The name simply means "a follower of Christ." "Christians, " in the New Testament, were "followers of Christ." The word *Christ* is simply a Greek version of the word *Messiah*, and there can be no question that Old Testament believers were followers of the Messiah.
[17] Hebrews 4:15, 2 Corinthians 5:21, 1 Peter 1:19
[18] E. G. White, *The Desire of Ages,* p. 25
[19] F. C. Gilbert, *Practical Lessons from the Experience of Israel*, (South Lancaster, Mass.: South Lancaster Printing Company, 1902), p. 189.
[20] John 1:1-11
[21] John 16:27
[22] Revelation 1:20

The Ark of the Covenant

In 1968, a Swiss-born hotel manager by the name of Erich Von Daniken published a book that quickly rocketed its way to the top of the best-seller list. In it, he suggested that the human race developed on earth as the result of experiments by extra-terrestrials who visited the planet thousands of years ago. The mysterious line drawings that spread for miles across the Nazca plains of Peru were said to be the remnants of a giant interstellar airfield. Ancient rock paintings from around the world were said to show us pictures of ancient space travelers. The "wheel within a wheel" that Ezekiel witnessed was described as a flying saucer.

Early in the book, Von Daniken offered his eager public an explanation for the design of the Ark of the Covenant:

Undoubtedly the Ark was electrically charged! If we reconstruct it today according to the instructions handed down by Moses, an electric conductor of several hundred volts is produced. The border and golden crown would have served to charge the condenser which was formed by the gold plates and a positive and negative conductor. If, in addition, one of the two cherubim on the mercy seat acted as a magnet, the loudspeaker—perhaps even a kind of set for communication between Moses and the spaceship—was perfect. The details of the construction of the Ark of the Covenant can be read in the Bible in their entirety. Without actually consulting Exodus, I seem to remember that the Ark

*was often surrounded by flashing sparks and that Moses made use of this
"transmitter" whenever he needed help and advice.*[23]

At least Mr. Von Daniken was honest enough to tell us that he hadn't
consulted the book of Exodus carefully! While the Ark *did* serve as a
place for communication, there is no mention in the Bible of "flashing
sparks" around the Ark. There is also no mention of magnets, condensers
or loudspeakers. Time and careful research have proven that *Chariots of
the Gods,* while published as a work of *non*fiction, is actually a masterful
work of *science* fiction.

In 1981, director Steven Spielberg's film *Raiders of the Lost Ark*
became an instant success at box offices across North America. It was
the fictitious story of an American archaeologist ("Indiana Jones")
who in 1936 was trying to find the location of the Ark of the Covenant
before the Nazis could discover it and tap into its mysterious powers.
The Germans, according to the plot of the movie, were eager to find the
Ark because of its supernatural ability to win wars for its possessor. Of
course, there is no historical record of Hitler trying to find the Ark to help
him win the war, but it made for great box office returns.

What these two accounts of the Ark underscore is the human race's
fascination with this ancient artifact. When you read the Bible's accounts
of the Ark, it becomes clear that there was *something* special about it.
Those among God's people who touched it or looked inside of it died
on the spot. When the Philistines put it in the temple of Dagon as a war
trophy, the statue of their god mysteriously fell over twice, and was
dismembered the second time. Their nation was overrun with rodents
and hit with a devastating plague of tumors until they got rid of it.

When Israelite priests carried the Ark of the Covenant into the Jordan
River, the waters were parted, creating a bridge of dry ground for the
people to pass through:

*...as those who bore the ark came to the Jordan, and the feet of the
priests who bore the ark dipped in the edge of the water (for the Jordan
overflows all its banks during the whole time of harvest), that the waters
which came down from upstream stood still, and rose in a heap very far
away at Adam, the city that is beside Zaretan. So the waters that went
down into the Sea of the Arabah, the Salt Sea, failed, and were cut off;
and the people crossed over opposite Jericho. Then the priests who bore
the ark of the covenant of the LORD stood firm on dry ground in the*

midst of the Jordan; and all Israel crossed over on dry ground, until all
the people had crossed completely over the Jordan. (Joshua 3:15-17)

After crossing the Jordan, the Israelites conquered the city of Jericho.
How did it happen? They carried the Ark of the Covenant around the
city once a day for six days, and on the seventh day, they circled the city
seven times and blew a trumpet. The walls of the city collapsed, making
it vulnerable to the Israelite army.[24]

The Ark was not an ordinary piece of furniture. There really *was*
something special about it. So if it wasn't an extraterrestrial commu-
nications machine, and it wasn't a source of secret power for the Nazis,
what exactly was it?

The book of Exodus gives us the earliest description of the Ark of the
Covenant. God told Moses to build it *exactly* according to the pattern he
was shown. It was a wooden chest overlaid with gold, about the size of a
standard office desk. The lid was made of solid gold, and has come to be
known as the *Mercy Seat.* It was graced by two golden cherubim, which
faced each other and looked reverently down upon the lid of the Ark. The
Ten Commandments, which had been etched in two tables of stone by
the finger of God Himself, were placed inside. Aaron's rod, which had
miraculously budded,[25] and a pot of manna[26] were also placed in the Ark,
but were later removed.

When the Ark was completed, it was placed in the innermost chamber
of the sanctuary, the Most Holy Place. This chamber then became the
very center of the camp of Israel, and the rest of the tabernacle was set
up around it. As the Israelites crossed the desert, the presence of God
led them; when the pillar of cloud and fire stopped moving, they pitched
camp and the presence of God would descend over the Most Holy Place
and take up residence above the Ark of the Covenant:

Whenever the cloud was taken up from above the tabernacle, the
children of Israel would go onward in all their journeys. But if the cloud
was not taken up, then they did not journey till the day that it was taken
up. For the cloud of the LORD was above the tabernacle by day, and fire
was over it by night, in the sight of all the house of Israel, throughout all
their journeys. (Exodus 40:36-38)

The Ark of the Covenant became a "throne" for the presence of God
among the Israelites. When God told Moses to build it, He informed
Moses that it would be from the vantage point of the Mercy Seat that He

would communicate His will to the nation of Israel:

"And there I will meet with you, and I will speak with you from above the mercy seat, from between the two cherubim which are on the ark of the Testimony, about everything which I will give you in commandment to the children of Israel." (Exodus 25:22)

As noted earlier in this book, God is often spoken of as "dwelling between the cherubim." The Ark in the earthly sanctuary was a model of God's throne in heaven—something that a number of prophets were privileged to see in vision. Both Ezekiel and Isaiah saw the throne of God in heaven, as did Daniel and the apostle John.[27] Then, in Revelation 11:19, we find specific mention of an *ark* in the courts of heaven:

Then the temple of God was opened in heaven, and the ark of His covenant was seen in His temple. And there were lightnings, noises, thunderings, an earthquake, and great hail. (Revelation 11:19)

As long as we are in the book of Revelation, let me point out an interesting connection between the last book of the Bible and the Old Testament sanctuary. Imagery from the tabernacle is used throughout John's apocalyptic prophecy:

• In **Revelation 1**, Jesus appears to John with seven golden candlesticks.

• In **Revelation 3**, Christ promises that those who overcome this world will be made into a "pillar in the temple of my God."

• In **Revelation 4**, there are seven lamps of fire burning before God's throne. There are also twenty-four elders, which some scholars feel correspond to the 24 courses of Levites that worked in the temple.

• In **Revelation 5**, Christ appears as a slain lamb.

• In **Revelation 7**, there is mention of the fact that those who experience great tribulation in this world will serve God in His temple.

• In **Revelation 8**, the Bible describes an angel offering incense on the "golden altar" before the throne of God.

• In **Revelation 11**, John is told to measure the temple of God and the altar, but not the courtyard. It is at the end of this chapter that he sees the ark of God's testament (or covenant) in heaven's temple.

• In **Revelation 14**, an angel comes out of the temple in heaven, prepared to reap the earth at the Second Coming of Christ.

• In **Revelation 15**, the temple of God in heaven is filled with smoke, making access impossible until the seven last plagues have been completed.

• In **Revelation 16**, a loud voice comes out of heaven's temple.

• In **Revelation 21**, the heavenly city is described as the "tabernacle of God" with men.

This is by no means an exhaustive list of allusions to the sanctuary in the book of Revelation. When you factor in all of the allusions to Old Testament sanctuary rituals, the list of references swells to staggering proportions. And in the midst of it, John sees the throne of God in heaven—an ark located in the temple in heaven.

The Ark of the Covenant teaches us something exceptionally important about Jesus Christ. As certain sacrificial animals were slaughtered, their blood was sprinkled on the veil that separated the Holy Place from the Most Holy Place.[28] This pointed to the fact that Jesus would one day present His own blood in the heavenly sanctuary as atonement for our sins. His sacrifice makes us acceptable in the presence of God, and opens the door for a relationship between the sinner and God:

Seeing then that we have a great High Priest who has passed through the heavens, Jesus the Son of God, let us hold fast our confession. For we do not have a High Priest who cannot sympathize with our weaknesses, but was in all points tempted as we are, yet without sin. Let us therefore come boldly to the throne of grace, that we may obtain mercy and find grace to help in time of need. (Hebrews 4:14-16)

Take a moment to think about the Ark as a symbol of the throne of God. The Ten Commandments were kept inside of it as a constant reminder that God's government is based on moral law. He is a *just* God. According to the Bible, sin is the transgression of the moral law,[29] and when a sinner approaches the throne of God he stands condemned by the moral law that rests in its foundation. The book of James also makes it clear that if we have broken even one law out of ten, we have broken them all and stand condemned by our actions.[30]

That is why the priest never actually went inside the Most Holy Place to stand in front of the Ark. (Only the High Priest could enter the innermost chamber once a year under very special circumstances.) Even though he represented Christ, he was still a sinful human being, incapable of standing in God's presence. All of us stand condemned by the fact that we have broken God's moral law:

For the wages of sin is death, but the gift of God is eternal life in Christ Jesus our Lord. (Romans 6:23)

One of the most important words in that verse is *but*. That one word takes a horrible situation—the wages of sin—and turns it on its head.

When I first got married I naturally wanted to do everything that I could to please my wife. One day, when she was out for the morning, I decided to make the bed. I actually *hate* making the bed, but I knew it would please her, so I gave it a try. When she came home, she saw what I had done, and she came to congratulate me on my effort.

"Honey, " she said, "that was really nice, *but...*"

What did that mean? It meant she would rather do the job herself next time! "But" changes everything! When the Bible says that the wages of sin is death, "but..." it means there is an alternative. You don't have to pay the death penalty for your sins because God has made a way of escape. We might stand condemned when we approach God's throne and the law inside of it, but resting over God's law is something known as the *mercy seat*.

The Ark of the Covenant teaches us that in addition to being perfectly just, God is also wonderfully merciful. The Psalmist captured this beautiful blending of justice and mercy in God's throne like this:

Surely His salvation is near to those who fear Him, that glory may dwell in our land. Mercy and truth have met together; righteousness and peace have kissed. (Psalm 85:9, 10)

In the Bible, the throne of God is often shown with a rainbow around it. The rainbow symbolizes God's mercy and His promise of salvation, which is evident from the fact that He gave the rainbow to Noah as a special sign after the flood. How do you create a rainbow? Mix rain with sunshine. Likewise, the mixture of God's justice and mercy paints a beautiful picture of His loving character.

As the blood of Christ is presented before the throne of God in heaven, you can rest in the knowledge that God is both perfectly just and perfectly merciful. The wages of your sins have been paid, satisfying the demands of justice; but Someone else has paid them for you in an act of unrivalled mercy. It is up to you whether or not you wish to accept the gift offered to you by heaven's High Priest. If He does not represent you in the courts of heaven, you must represent yourself, and you have nothing to bring to the throne of God except a long track record of violating God's law.

In 1830, a man by the name of George Wilson killed a government employee who caught him in the act of robbing the United States mail. Wilson was later apprehended for the crime, and the courts condemned him to die for his crime by hanging.

For some reason, President Andrew Jackson heard about the case, and was moved to offer Wilson a pardon. Most people on death row would jump at the chance of forgiveness and release, but George Wilson did a very strange thing. He refused to accept it. He didn't *want* to be forgiven.

Nobody had ever heard of someone on death row turning down a presidential pardon, and nobody was quite sure what to do about it. The case was referred to the U.S. Supreme Court, which came to a precedent-setting decision delivered by Chief Justice Marshall:

"A pardon is a slip of paper, the value of which is determined by the acceptance of the person to be pardoned. If it is refused, it is no pardon. George Wilson must be hanged."

To refuse your heavenly pardon is a tragedy of the highest order. There is nothing you can do to earn your salvation; that is why Christ gave His life for you. Now He stands in heaven's sanctuary, offering to cover your sins with His blood—a gift from God Himself. A lot of people simply pass up the offer. They are not interested in a pardon from God's mercy seat. They're confident that they will somehow work things out on their own. Eventually, everyone is going to face the throne of God:

For we shall all stand before the judgment seat of Christ. For it is written: "As I live, says the LORD, every knee shall bow to Me, and every tongue shall confess to God." So then each of us shall give account of himself to God. (Romans 14:10b-12)

There is only one hope of surviving your encounter with the perfect throne of God—you need Christ to stand in your place. In the Old Testament, we discover that anybody who touched the Ark paid for it with his life—and that is because sinful human beings are unable to stand in the presence of God. But Christ is sinless, and He already paid for your transgressions. He *can* touch the Ark, and He is willing to do it for you.

If you were to stand before God's throne today, how would you fare? When Christ carries His blood into heaven's sanctuary, is He representing you? "If we confess our sins," the Bible says, "He is faithful and just to forgive us our sins and to cleanse us from all unrighteousness." (1 John 1:9)

In light of what happened in the Old Testament sanctuary, and remembering the fact that it represented the ministry of Christ in heaven's sanctuary for you, consider the words that close the book of Jude:

Now to Him who is able to keep you from stumbling, and to present you faultless before the presence of His glory with exceeding joy, to God our Savior, who alone is wise, be glory and majesty, dominion and power, both now and forever. Amen. (Jude 1:24, 25)

---

[23] Von Daniken, *Chariots of the Gods,* p. 40.
[24] Joshua 6
[25] Numbers 17:7-10; Hebrews 9:4
[26] Hebrews 9:4
[27] Ezekiel 1; Isaiah 6; Daniel 7; Revelation 4, 5
[28] See, for example, Leviticus 4:4-7, 16-18
[29] 1 John 3:4
[30] James 2:8-10

CHAPTER EIGHT

Immanuel

The children of Israel had been slaves in Babylon for decades. The city of Jerusalem, with its magnificent temple, lay in ruins. Centuries ago, their father Abraham had been led by God out of Babylonian territory into the Promised Land, but now they found themselves subjected to the humiliation of being sent back where they started. The Babylonian captivity was more than simple subjection to a foreign army; it was a message from God that He was chastising His unfaithful bride by returning her to the place of her origin:

"And I will judge you as women who break wedlock or shed blood are judged; I will bring blood upon you in fury and jealousy. I will also give you into their hand, and they shall throw down your shrines and break down your high places. They shall also strip you of your clothes, take your beautiful jewelry, and leave you naked and bare. They shall also bring up an assembly against you, and they shall stone you with stones and thrust you through with their swords. They shall burn your houses with fire, and execute judgments on you in the sight of many women; and I will make you cease playing the harlot, and you shall no longer hire lovers."[31] *(Ezekiel 16:38-41)*

What was the crime of Israel? Even though the Ark of the Covenant was in their midst, and they had a clear picture of God's desire to save them, they still chose to ignore Him and chase after other gods.

Additionally, the Sabbath day, a symbol of God's special relationship with His people, was routinely ignored in favor of personal pursuits:

"But if you will not heed Me to hallow the Sabbath day, such as not carrying a burden when entering the gates of Jerusalem on the Sabbath day, then I will kindle a fire in its gates, and it shall devour the palaces of Jerusalem, and it shall not be quenched." (Jeremiah 17:27)

The whole identity of the nation was demolished as the armies of Nebuchadnezzar fulfilled this prophecy and sacked the city. Even though the destruction of Jerusalem had been prophesied, most were still surprised by the event, because they refused to believe that God would ever let anything happen to the temple. False prophets had tried to temper Jeremiah's warnings, repeatedly urging people to remember "the temple of the Lord, the temple of the Lord, the temple of the Lord." (Jeremiah 7:4)

Many people could point to the fact that God had stopped the plague (brought on by David's disobedience) from destroying the city of Jerusalem.[32] They could stand on the fact that Hezekiah had managed to stave off the armies of Sennacherib, even after Samaria had fallen. The temple was stripped of some of its wealth to pay tribute, but it was not destroyed;[33] neither was Jerusalem. Mount Zion, after all, is where God *desired* to make His home.[34]

"This is where God's presence dwells!" they protested. "Nothing's going to happen!"

They had forgotten what happened to the Israelites during the time Eli had compromised His commitment to the Lord. They carried the Ark of the Covenant into battle against the Philistines; those who survived came home without it. The Ark was not a magical charm bracelet that brought its possessors good luck; its power was rooted in the covenant relationship the descendants of Abraham had with God. Once the covenant relationship had been broken, and Israel turned their backs on God, the presence of the Ark was of little benefit to them. God pled with them to change their ways:

Thus says the LORD of hosts, the God of Israel: "Amend your ways and your doings, and I will cause you to dwell in this place. Do not trust in these lying words, saying, 'The temple of the LORD, the temple of the LORD, the temple of the LORD are these.' For if you thoroughly amend your ways and your doings, if you thoroughly execute judgment between a man and his neighbor, if you do not oppress the stranger, the fatherless, and the widow, and do not shed innocent blood in this place, or walk after other gods to your hurt, then I will cause you to dwell in this place, in the land that I gave to your fathers forever and ever. Behold, you trust in lying words that cannot profit. Will you steal, murder, commit adultery, swear falsely, burn incense to Baal, and walk after other gods whom you do not know, and then come and stand before Me in this house which is called by My name, and say, 'We are delivered to do all these abominations'? Has this house, which is called by My name, become a den of thieves in your eyes? Behold, I, even I, have seen it," says the LORD. (Jeremiah 7:3-11)

In spite of repeated warnings from God, Israel refused to give up her other gods, and so the presence of God left the city of Jerusalem,[35] and the city was left for the Babylonians to conquer. Through the prophet Jeremiah, the Israelites were informed that the Babylonian captivity would last for 70 years.

Those 70 hard years were now drawing to a close, and it was time for Israel to return home and rebuild the temple. There wasn't much evidence, however, to suggest that anything was about to happen. Babylon was still strong. They were still captives.

And then suddenly, an army led by the Persian general Cyrus surrounded the city. Was this to be the moment of their deliverance?

The Babylonian king didn't think so. Israel was not the only nation that had trouble believing that the God of heaven is able to bring a kingdom to its knees. When the Persian armies surrounded the city, Belshazzar decided to throw a party. After all, he assured himself, the walls of Babylon were high enough to prevent Cyrus from scaling them, and they were too thick to break through.

When Cyrus first arrived the Babylonian army was waiting for him. But it didn't go well for the Babylonians. They were soundly defeated and forced to retreat into the city—yet, they still weren't worried because the city itself was their biggest advantage. There were enough provisions inside the walls to last for years, and the Euphrates River ran right through the middle of the city providing a perpetual source of water. They could wait out a very lengthy siege. The ancient historian Herodotus tells the story like this:

The Babylonians had taken the field and were awaiting his approach.

When he arrived near the city they attacked him, but were defeated and forced to retire inside their defences; they already knew of Cyrus' restless ambition and had watched his successive acts of aggression against one nation after another, and as they had taken the precaution of accumulating in Babylon a stock of provisions sufficient to last many years, they were able to regard the prospect of a siege with indifference. The siege dragged on, no progress was made, and Cyrus was beginning to despair of success.[36]

Human beings have a destructive habit of ignoring the plain word of God. If the tangible evidence around us seems to suggest that God might be wrong, we quickly run to stand on it. Take, for example, the current trend to accept the theory of evolution as scientific fact when the Bible tells us otherwise. Even though scientific evidence for the theory is actually quite scanty, we seem eager to accept it because if you can reject the theory of creation, you can ignore much of the other counsel the Bible gives that would affect the way you live your life.

Another good example is the recent discovery of the *Gospel of Judas*, a Gnostic document discovered in Egypt in the 1970s. In 2006, the manuscript was paraded on the nightly news as possible evidence that the biblical gospels were not telling the truth. There is no evidence to suggest that the *Gospel of Judas* contains an authentic account of the life of Christ, and the biblical account has more evidence to support its authenticity—by far—than any other ancient document in existence. Still, many are quick to run to something that might serve to dismiss the claims that God has on our lives. That is what makes the regurgitated mythology of books like *The Da Vinci Code* so appealing to us.

The city of Babylon made a science out of willful ignorance. The prophet Daniel had lived in their midst throughout the years of the captivity, and the Babylonians had received ample warning that the city would not stand forever. Nebuchadnezzar had been shown in a dream that his empire would give way to an inferior kingdom.[37] He had also been shown—in no uncertain terms—that the God of heaven, Who had permitted him to build his expansive empire, was willing and able to take it away on a moment's notice.[38] Daniel had been shown, with vivid detail, that the bear of Medo-Persia would destroy the lion of Babylon.[39] Jeremiah, prophet to the Israelite captives, had produced a specific timeline for the return to Jerusalem: 70 years.[40]

Still, Belshazzar couldn't bring himself to accept that the Persians would take the city. The walls of the city were, after all, a formidable barrier. He chose to place his faith in them, and to prove his point, he threw a party to reassure his people that nothing could possibly go wrong:

Belshazzar the king made a great feast for a thousand of his lords, and drank wine in the presence of the thousand. While he tasted the wine, Belshazzar gave the command to bring the gold and silver vessels which his father Nebuchadnezzar had taken from the temple which had been in Jerusalem, that the king and his lords, his wives, and his concubines might drink from them... (Daniel 5:1, 2)

The sacred vessels from the temple in Jerusalem—spoils from past military victories—were brought out as proof that Babylon was invincible. In her moment of greatest peril Babylon chose to ignore the armies at the gate, and got drunk instead.

Babylon has become a potent symbol for the human race living at the end of time. The book of Revelation describes a last-day *spiritual* Babylon that is also drunk. The "inhabitants of the earth have been made drunk with the wine of her fornication,"[41] and her citizens refuse to accept the reality that Babylon will fall. Then, suddenly, it happens:

"The merchants of these things, who became rich by her, will stand at a distance for fear of her torment, weeping and wailing, and saying, 'Alas, alas, that great city that was clothed in fine linen, purple, and scarlet, and adorned with gold and precious stones and pearls! For in one hour such great riches came to nothing.' Every shipmaster, all who travel by ship, sailors, and as many as trade on the sea, stood at a distance and cried out when they saw the smoke of her burning, saying, 'What is like this great city?' They threw dust on their heads and cried out, weeping and wailing, and saying, 'Alas, alas, that great city, in which all who had ships on the sea became rich by her wealth! For in one hour she is made desolate.'" (Revelation 18:15-19)

The stories of the Bible are not just a record of ancient history. God Himself carefully chose them as object lessons for future generations. The story of Babylon's collapse at the hands of the Persians is a prediction for our generation. The details give us a picture of things to come.

Notice, for example, that the Persians were not just an invading army. They were the agents chosen by God to bring His people back to the Promised Land. The prophet Isaiah called Cyrus "God's anointed,"[42] because he was the One who would allow Israel to return to Jerusalem and rebuild the sacred temple.

Likewise, when last-day Babylon falls, it will happen in conjunction with the Second Coming of Christ. Jesus, the Anointed One, will return to this world with the armies of heaven to liberate His people from the captivity they have had to endure in this world. They are then free to return to the heavenly Promised Land and to heaven's sanctuary.

As Belshazzar and his men became more and more drunk that night, Cyrus was busy laying plans. He had learned something valuable on his way to Babylon:

On his march to Babylon Cyrus came to the river Gyndes which rises in the Matienian mountains, runs through the country of the Dardanes and then joins the Tigris which passes the city of Opis and flows into the Persian Gulf. Cyrus was preparing to cross this river, for which boats were needed, when one of his sacred white horses, a high-spirited creature, entered the water and attempted to swim across but was swept under by the rapid current and carried away. Cyrus was so furious with the river for daring to do such a thing, that he swore he would punish it by making it so weak that even a woman could get over in the future without difficulty and without wetting her knees. He held up his march against Babylon, divided his army into two parts, marked out on each side of the river a hundred and eighty channels running off from it in various directions, and ordered his men to set to work and dig. Having a vast number of hands employed, he managed to finish the job, but only at the cost of the whole summer wasted. Then, having punished the Gyndes by splitting it into three hundred and sixty separate channels, Cyrus, at the beginning of the following spring, resumed his march to Babylon.[43]

The ancient historian says that Cyrus "wasted" his summer to tame the Gyndes; sacred history proves that it was a valuable lesson and the key to Babylon's overthrow. He stationed soldiers at both ends of the river as it went into and came out of the city.

He told them to enter the city as soon as the water level was low enough to make it possible. Then he took his non-combatant workforce upstream to a place where someone had already created a lake by diverting the Euphrates some years before. The lake was now nearly empty; Cyrus reopened the channel that had once filled it, and the water in the Euphrates began to drop. That night, drunk Babylon fell—just the way God said it would.

The Israelites eventually made their way back to the ruined city of Jerusalem, where they began to rebuild the city and the temple. As the temple neared completion, however, there was one small problem. The Ark of the Covenant was missing.

It is still missing to this day. In spite of a number of people who claimed to have found it shortly after the release of *Raiders of the Lost Ark*, its whereabouts have never been discovered (or at least confirmed). Some say that it is hidden on the west bank of the Jordan near the Dead Sea. Still others claim that it is located under Mount Calvary or in a system of tunnels under the temple mount.

One proposal that has gained some popularity in recent years suggests that the Ark is now housed in a church located in the city of Axum, Ethiopia. How did it get that far from home? A historical legend suggests it went to Ethiopia with a son born to King Solomon and the Queen of Sheba named Menelik. According to legend, the wise Israelite king created a replica of the Ark for his son to take back to Ethiopia. But the arks were covertly switched, and today the real Ark is still located in Africa. This story has been widely promoted by the Falashas, a tribe in Ethiopia that has adhered to the Jewish faith since antiquity.[44]

One fascinating theory as to its fate is found in the apocryphal book of Second Maccabees. While this book is not inspired scripture, it does give us a good account of Jewish history. It indicates that the prophet Jeremiah hid the Ark in a cave on Mount Nebo to save it from being captured by the Babylonian hordes:

We find in the archives that the prophet Jeremiah...warned by an oracle, gave orders for the tabernacle and the ark to go with him when he set out for the mountain which Moses had climbed to survey God's heritage. On his arrival Jeremiah found a cave dwelling, into which he brought the tabernacle, the ark and the altar of incense, afterward blocking up the entrance. Some of his companions came up to mark out the way, but were unable to find it. When Jeremiah learned this, he reproached them: "The place is to remain unknown," he said, "until God gathers his people together again and shows them his mercy. Then the Lord will bring these things once more to light, and the glory of the Lord will be seen, and so will the cloud, as it was revealed in the time of Moses and when Solomon prayed that the Holy Place might be gloriously hallowed."[45]

The truth is, nobody really knows. At the time of this writing, we still haven't found the Ark of the Covenant, even though there are hundreds of theories as to its whereabouts. The point is that the Israelites didn't have an Ark to place in the Temple when they rebuilt it, which must have been a real source of heartache for a people who had been accustomed to having God's presence among them. They knew that when Solomon built the first temple and dedicated it, the presence of God had filled the Most Holy Place:

When Solomon had finished praying, fire came down from heaven and consumed the burnt offering and the sacrifices; and the glory of the LORD filled the temple. And the priests could not enter the house of the LORD, because the glory of the LORD had filled the LORD's house. (2 Chronicles 7:1, 2)

This didn't happen when the second temple was built. The prophet Ezra simply records that the Israelites finished building the Temple and then they dedicated it. No fire fell from heaven to consume the sacrifices. The presence of God did not fill the Most Holy Place. All through the building process, there were people who had complained about the inferiority of the new temple, and now the Divine Presence had failed to come. It was a crushing blow for a lot of God's people.

But in the midst of their disappointment, God gave them hope. In the second chapter of Haggai, we read a remarkable prophecy that the new temple would be more glorious than the first one:

"'The glory of this latter temple shall be greater than the former,' says the LORD of hosts. 'And in this place I will give peace,' says the LORD of hosts." (Haggai 2:9)

At the time, that must have been hard for a lot of people to believe. If the new Temple was going to be more glorious, why didn't they have the Ark of the Covenant? And where was the presence of God? Again, human evidence suggested that prophecy was wrong, because the Shekinah glory never again filled the Most Holy Place. Yet the seventh verse of this same prophecy says something very important:

And I will shake all the nations; and the desire of all nations shall come; and I will fill this house with glory, says the LORD of hosts. (Haggai 2:7, MKJV)

The new temple *would* be blessed with the glory of God. Someone called "the desire of all nations" would come and bless it with His presence. This was the same Person who created Adam and Eve and met them in the cool of the evening. He was the One who met with Abraham and promised him that his descendants would inherit the city of God, and the same One who led the children of Israel across the desert in a pillar of cloud. He came to the new Temple, not as a fiery presence, but as a *human being*. In a move that staggers the imagination, the barrier of the veil was set aside, and God wrapped himself in human flesh—just as the prophet Isaiah predicted would happen:

"Therefore the Lord Himself will give you a sign: Behold, the virgin shall conceive and bear a Son, and shall call His name Immanuel." (Isaiah 7:14)

Immanuel is a very important name. According to Matthew 1:23, it means "God with us." The birth of Christ is the ultimate expression of God's desire to dwell among His people. No longer did He reside on the other side of the veil where human eyes could not see Him. No longer did He speak to us from between the cherubim on the Ark of the Covenant. He had become a real flesh-and-blood human being. From this point on, He was not just *among* us; He was *one of us*—God in the flesh.

He taught in the temple where people could hear the voice of God for themselves. When sinful human beings couldn't cross the veil to visit God in the Most Holy Place, God stepped through the veil to visit them. That act of love—stepping down from the throne of heaven to humble Himself with human existence—made the new Temple a much more special place than the old one, because we were able to literally reach out and touch God.

The great Christian writer, C. S. Lewis, described the marvel of Christ's incarnation like this:

Imagine, for the moment, that your dog and every dog is in deep distress. Some of us love dogs very much. If it would help all the dogs in the world to become like men, would you be willing to become a dog? Would you put down your human nature, leave your loved ones, your job, hobbies, your art and literature and music, and choose instead of the intimate communion with your beloved, the poor substitute of looking into the beloved's face and wagging your tail, unable to smile or speak?[46]

Imagine leaving the courts of heaven for this world, with all of its trouble and sorrow. Imagine giving up streets of gold for a pair of sandals and long, hot dusty highways. Imagine giving up millions of adoring angels who love to perform your every wish for a group of self-satisfied sinners who would use Jesus' own words against Him in a plot to have Him killed. The book of Philippians says that Jesus "made Himself of no reputation, taking the form of a servant, and coming in the likeness of men." (Philippians 2:7)

Here is the stunning part—Jesus' decision to take on human nature was permanent. After the resurrection Jesus appeared to His disciples and encouraged them to touch the wounds in His hands and feet so that they would know beyond the shadow of a doubt that He was real. Then, when Jesus ascended into heaven with a *real human body*, the angels told the disciples that the *same* Jesus would return in glory. That means that He has chosen to permanently identify Himself with our race. Even though the Bible clearly identifies Him as the Creator, He has chosen to become a part of the creation. Could anything better underscore His desire to be among us?

The story is told of an ancient Persian king who loved his people very much. Looking out across his empire, he suddenly found himself wanting to be one of his own subjects. He wanted to know what it was like to face their hardships every day. So, periodically, he would put on a poor man's clothes and visit the homes of the poor. Of course, nobody recognized him when he dressed like a beggar.

One day, he visited a very poor man who lived in a cellar. He shared a meal with the man, and ate humble food that would never be allowed on the royal banquet table. After the meal, he tried his best to encourage this man and give him hope.

Then, at the end of the day, he left for home. Later on, he returned to see his new friend, and, on this occasion, he revealed his secret identity. "I'm not who you think I am," he said, pulling off his ragged cloak, "I'm actually your king!"

The king assumed that once his identity had been revealed, the poor man would ask him for money or some extravagant favor, but he was surprised by the response. "You left your palace and glory to visit me in this dark, dreary place," the beggar said, "and you ate the same lousy food I ate. That brings me a lot of joy. You have given money and gifts to other people, but you've given me something much better. You have given me yourself!"

That is the beauty of *Immanuel*. The tragedy is that we didn't appreciate what God had given us in the birth of Jesus Christ:

In Him was life, and the life was the light of men. And the light shines in the darkness, and the darkness did not comprehend it. (John 1:4, 5)

A little further on, John says this:

He was in the world, and the world was made through Him, and the world did not know Him. He came to His own, and His own did not receive Him. (John 1:10, 11)

Just imagine: when we could no longer step into the presence of God, He still did everything possible to place His presence among us. In the Old Testament, He pitched His tabernacle among His people so that we could be near Him. In the New Testament, He became one of us. Yet we refused to accept it. In fact, we found Him offensive and nailed Him to a cross.

Who would blame God if He simply abandoned or destroyed us? We didn't deserve the plan of salvation in the first place, yet, in the face of our rebellion and stubbornness, He persisted in loving us. Even as He hung on the cross, Jesus prayed, "Father, forgive them, for they do not know what they do." (Luke 23:32)

God took our supreme moment of rebellion, as we hung His Son on a cross to die, and turned it into His most glorious moment of love. We had sunk to our absolute lowest. We took a loving Creator whose greatest desire is to be with His people, and we treated Him in the most shameful manner possible. We treated Him as if He were not even worthy of our contempt. And still He loves us. God took what seemed like humiliating defeat and turned it into unparalleled triumph. As Jesus died on the cross of Calvary He became the sacrificial lamb of the Old Testament sanctuary service. The cross became the Altar of Sacrifice in the outer courtyard. And His blood, which He carried back to heaven with Him, became the blood that the Old Testament priests carried inside the Holy Place. The death of Christ became the solution for our rejection of Him.

At the moment Christ died, the veil in the temple was torn in two, exposing the Most Holy Place:

Then, behold, the veil of the temple was torn in two from top to bottom; and the earth quaked, and the rocks were split. (Matt. 27:51)

The earthly temple was no longer needed, because the Lamb of God had come to fulfill what the temple services had been designed to predict. In later years, the Romans came and utterly destroyed the temple as Jesus predicted.[47] It has never been rebuilt. We simply don't need it anymore. When Jesus became our sacrificial lamb, our focus moved from the earthly tabernacle to the heavenly sanctuary:

For Christ has not entered the holy places made with hands, which are copies of the true, but into heaven itself, now to appear in the presence of God for us. (Hebrews 9:24)

There are people who still anticipate that the temple in Jerusalem will be rebuilt one day. In fact, some even say it is necessary for the fulfillment of Bible prophecy and must happen before Christ can return. I found a great example of this theory in a popular book on Bible prophecy:

Anyone interested in end-time events has his eyes on the temple project. Ever since the Jews took temporary possession of the temple site after the Six Day War in 1967, there have been rumors that various groups have been working clandestinely to prepare all the materials it needs—from the robes of the priests to the tapestry in the temple. I have even heard reports that all the elaborate worship utensils have been prefabricated in preparation for the day that permission is granted to begin construction of the third temple. There have been reports that a detailed model of the temple has been traveling throughout the United States to raise money for the project. That would make sense, for almost 50 percent of world's Jewry lives in America, and doubtless the richest Jews in the world reside in this country. American Jews have a long history of providing generous donations to the needs and causes of fellow Jews, particularly those in Israel.[48]

Those who adhere rigidly to this theory insist that if the Antichrist is going to desecrate the temple during the Tribulation period, the temple must first be rebuilt. This is, unfortunately, a misunderstanding of Bible prophecy that takes an important ancient prediction and breaks it into two pieces without any support in the biblical text for doing so. In the chapter entitled *The Judgment Hour* we will explore this prophecy in more detail, and discover what many people have failed to notice. But for now, the question is simple: will it happen?

Will the Ark of the Covenant be rediscovered and placed back in a newly built temple? It's hard to say. Given the climate in the Middle

East, it is not unimaginable that the temple could be rebuilt. I suppose that it is even possible that the Ark could be rediscovered. But one thing is abundantly clear in the pages of the Bible: *we don't need a temple on earth any more.* God will never re-establish the Old Testament sacrificial system, because the One it was designed to reveal is now our High Priest in the *real* sanctuary, located in heaven.

The sanctuary *does* have something to say about the last days, however. In addition to the animals that were offered on a daily basis, there were seven annual celebrations that paint an unbelievable picture of the earth's final moments. As we look at them, you might just want to buckle your seatbelts.

---

[31] Ezekiel 16 gives us God's perspective on Israel at this period of history. He describes her as a helpless baby girl that He took into His home and gave all of the advantages of life. When she was old enough, He married her, but she proved to be unfaithful to Him – so He strips her of privilege and turns her away. Lamentations 1:10-12 indicates that Israel understood the humiliation of this event.

[32] 1 Chronicles 21

[33] 2 Kings 18:13-16

[34] Psalm 132:13

[35] Ezekiel 10 is a vivid description of God leaving the temple in Jerusalem. Verses 18 and 19 indicate a final departure of His presence.

[36] Herodotus, *The Histories*, Book One, 190

[37] Daniel 2

[38] Daniel 4

[39] Daniel 7

[40] 2 Chronicles 36:21

[41] Revelation 17:3. See also Revelation 17:6; 18:3

[42] See Isaiah 44:27-45:1 for an amazing prophecy of the fall of Babylon given more than 100 years before Cyrus' birth.

[43] Herodotus, *The Histories,* Book One, 189.

[44] See the following works, which are referenced www.christiananswers.net in an article by Gary Byers: (1) Fisher, Milton C. 1995. "The Ark of the Covenant: Alive and Well in Ethiopia?" *Bible and Spade* 8/3, pp. 65-72. (2) Hancock, Graham. 1992. *The Sign and the Seal: The Quest for the Lost Ark of the Covenant*. New York: Crown Books.

[45] 2 Maccabees 2:1-8

[46] C.S. Lewis, posted at http://www.sermonillustrations.com

[47] Matthew 23:37-24:2

[48] Tim LaHaye, et al., *Are We Living in the End Times?* (Wheaton, Illinois: Tyndale House, 1999), p. 124.

CHAPTER NINE

Dinner Jackets Required

It is a spring night in the land of ancient Goshen. The ripening grain is quietly waving under a full moon and the day's work is finished. Everyone is safely at home. The smell of freshly baked bread and roast lamb fills the air. It's like the close of any other workday, except for one unusual detail. Everyone is eating with his or her coats on—and they have their sandals on, too. The father of each family is holding a walking staff in his hand as he eats his dinner. It's as if they are planning to dine and dash.

Suddenly, the quiet of the night is pierced by the horrified shriek of a mother who has just found the body of her oldest son, stiff and cold in his bed. Then a cry goes up from the neighbor's house. They have made the same discovery. Something—or *somebody*—is taking the lives of all the oldest sons. But it is only true in the homes of Egyptians.

Why were the Israelite homes untouched? The Bible record reveals the secret:

Then Moses called for all the elders of Israel and said to them, "Pick out and take lambs for yourselves according to your families, and kill the Passover lamb. And you shall take a bunch of hyssop, dip it in the blood that is in the basin, and strike the lintel and the two doorposts with the blood that is in the basin. And none of you shall go out of the door of his house until morning. For the LORD will pass through to strike

the Egyptians; and when He sees the blood on the lintel and on the two
doorposts, the LORD will pass over the door and not allow the destroyer
to come into your houses to strike you." (Exodus 12:21-23)

God told the Israelites to go on the tenth day of the month and
choose a lamb for a special ceremony. Not just any old lamb—it had to
be the very best they had. It had to be perfect, without the slightest little
blemish. It was to be set aside until the fourteenth day of the same month,
when it would be slaughtered and eaten.

In addition to eating the lamb, the Israelites were to take its blood and
smear it over the doorposts of their homes. This way, God told them, the
destroying angel would "pass over" their houses and move on to the next
one. That is the reason, of course, that we still call the annual celebration
of that night the *Passover.* The plague of death had "passed over" God's
people and left them completely unharmed.

It doesn't take a lot of imagination to see what God was trying to
teach His people through this ritual. Jesus is the innocent Lamb of God,
and as we accept the death of Christ in our behalf, and smear the blood
of His gift on the doorposts of our hearts, it renders us immune to the
ultimate plague of death—the wages of sin.

That is the simplest understanding of the Passover celebration. The
imagery takes us much further, however. After the lamb's blood was
sprinkled on the doorpost, the family roasted and ate the lamb along with
unleavened bread and bitter herbs. If there was any meat left over at the
end of the meal it had to be destroyed in the fire, because, as the symbol
of Christ, under no circumstance could it be allowed to spoil.

This requirement clearly points us to Jesus, and His sacrifice on the
cross. Even though He passed through death for us, His body did not
decompose in the grave. Instead, He rose on the third day. A stunning
prophecy in the sixteenth Psalm predicted this:

For You will not leave my soul in Sheol,[49] nor will You allow Your
Holy One to see corruption. (Psalm 16:10)

The more you study the Passover Lamb, the more it points you to
Jesus. After the first Passover, the Israelites continued to celebrate it
every year in the spring. On the tenth day of the Hebrew month of Nisan,
they chose a lamb to be slaughtered. They killed it on the fourteenth day.
During the four days between selection and the slaughter, the lamb was
usually tied to a stake so the public could examine it, making sure that it

really was a *perfect* lamb.

That timing appears to have been very important. When Jesus entered the city of Jerusalem on a donkey,[50] it was the ninth day of the month, or five days before the Passover. At some point after that, according to Luke's gospel,[51] Jesus drove the moneychangers out of the temple and began to teach there for the public to hear.

At first glance, it seems a little odd that Jesus would spend so much time teaching in the public eye when He knew that the authorities were intent on destroying Him, but in light of the lessons of Passover, it's not strange at all. It is likely that Jesus taught publicly in the temple from the tenth day of the month until the day that He was crucified on the fourteenth.

Just like the Passover lamb, He was on public display—for four days—so that anyone who wanted to inspect Him could. They could hear His teachings and judge for themselves whether or not He was a pure and spotless Lamb.

In fact, when Jesus was on trial before Annas, the former High Priest, Annas told Jesus to explain Himself. Jesus answered that He had been in the temple teaching publicly, and that if Annas wanted to know what He had said, He could go and ask the people who heard Him.[52] Just like the Passover Lamb, Jesus had been on public display long enough for everyone to know that He really was the perfect Lamb of God.

In conjunction with the Passover, the children of Israel celebrated the Feast of Unleavened Bread. Author F. C. Gilbert, writing in the early twentieth century, summarized the events associated with its celebration like this:

On the evening of the fourteenth of Nisan, the master of the house with one of his boys, generally the youngest, searches the house for leaven. Some time earlier in the day small pieces of bread are scattered in different rooms and halls of the house, wherever leaven of any kind has been used during the year. In the evening the man of the house generally takes a lighted candle, and goes in search of the leaven. The son carries the candle, while the parent has a feather and a wooden spoon. Each place or corner is very carefully scrutinized, and every piece is gathered up with great precision, so that not a particle of leaven may be left anywhere in the house. Before this is done, all work and study must be put aside, and necessary preparations made. When this is finished the pieces of leaven are securely tied, and placed somewhere in an unused part of the house; they are removed the next morning about ten, and burned. This is known as "removing" or "purging" the leaven. It is very punctiliously observed, and great care is taken that not one particle of the leaven remains.[53]

The bread eaten at Passover could have no leaven in it. Why? Leavening agents are used in the Bible to describe the effects of sin. This is why Paul told us to remove the "leaven" from our lives:

Your glorying is not good. Do you not know that a little leaven leavens the whole lump? Therefore purge out the old leaven, that you may be a new lump, since you truly are unleavened. For indeed Christ, our Passover, was sacrificed for us. Therefore let us keep the feast, not with old leaven, nor with the leaven of malice and wickedness, but with the unleavened bread of sincerity and truth. (1 Corinthians 5:6-8)

Jesus is sinless; therefore, the Passover bread could have no leaven in it, and the house had to be purged of all leavening agents. Sin has no place in the kingdom of Christ. It had no part in His life, and His sacrifice in our behalf removes the stain of sin from our lives as well.

Our perfect Passover Lamb is Jesus. When John the Baptist first saw Him, he said, "Behold the Lamb of God who takes away the sin of the world!"[54] In his first letter to the Corinthian church, Paul calls Jesus "our Passover," and says that He was sacrificed for us.[55] Peter said that Jesus was the perfect lamb without blemish or spot.[56] In the book of Revelation John sees Jesus enter the courts of heaven as a Lamb that was slain.[57]

God invites us to sprinkle the blood of Jesus on the doorposts of our hearts and minds. He gave His blood so that you and I could escape the plague of death and enjoy eternity in His presence. It is a gift of immeasurable worth.

Little Mary desperately needed a blood transfusion. She had a very rare disease, and her only chance of survival was to get blood from someone who had already had the disease and survived it. As luck would have it, her older brother Timmy fit the bill perfectly. Two worried parents took the their children to the hospital, where the doctor interviewed little Timmy.

"Listen, Timmy," he said, "I have an important question for you, and I want you to think it over very carefully. Would you be willing to give your blood for your sister?"

The room fell deathly quiet. The little boy didn't say anything for a moment, and his lower lip started to tremble, as if he were going to cry. Someone was just about to say something to relieve the tension in the room when suddenly the trembling lip gave way to a big smile. "Sure doctor," Timmy said, "for my sister, I'll do it!"

The two children were wheeled into a hospital room—pale, sickly Mary alongside her healthy big brother. Neither of them spoke a single word, but at one moment, their eyes suddenly met across the room. Timmy flashed a big, reassuring smile at his sister. She smiled back.

His smile started to fade, however, when a nurse pushed a needle into his arm. He watched the blood flow through a tube in grim silence for a few minutes, and then he asked to see the doctor. The doctor was brought in.

"What is it, Timmy?"

"Doctor," he said gravely, "when am I going to die?"

Why had Timmy hesitated in the beginning to give his blood? He thought he was going to have to give it *all*. To save his sister, he believed he was going to have to die.

"Greater love hath no man that this," said Jesus, "that a man lay down his life for his friends."[58] Our Passover Lamb was willing to give everything to save us for the kingdom. Not only was He willing to shed His blood, He was willing to die so that we could be free from the plague of death and the slavery of sin. I like the way that Christian author Martha Zimmerman puts it:

God sacrificed the Lamb on the altar of the Cross. Those wooden beams became the doorpost of the world's home. God promises to pass over us with His judgment of death as we are willing to stand under its protection. This is what we remember and celebrate at Passover.[59]

Isaiah, the gospel prophet, predicted the crucifixion of Christ in language that points us to the Passover:

He was oppressed and He was afflicted, yet He opened not His mouth; He was led as a lamb to the slaughter, And as a sheep before its shearers is silent, so He opened not His mouth. (Isaiah 53:7)

A slaughterhouse can be a terrible place. When the animals figure out what's actually happening, many of them begin to squeal in protest. It has been observed by some people, however, that a lamb is different. It will often face its fate without protest.

I don't know that to be true from personal experience, but if it is, perhaps that is one of the reasons God chose the innocent lamb to represent His Son. When Jesus appeared in the judgment hall, He refused to fight back. They spit on Him, they whipped Him, they made fun of Him, and they pulled the beard out of His face, but He never fought back. He knew that if you and I were going to be safe in the presence of God, there was no other way. Out of a love that is hard for us to understand, He went quietly to His fate.

I sometimes wonder, however, how the angels managed to keep silent when Jesus went to the cross. What held them back when we whipped the back of God's perfect Son with a crude Roman whip? Who stopped them from annihilating us when we drove the nails into Christ's hands and shoved the spear through His side? How could they just stand by and do *nothing*?

Revelation 13:8 reveals that Jesus is the "lamb slain from the foundation of the world." The plan of salvation was organized right from the very beginning of creation. Before we ever fell into sin, Jesus volunteered to be our Passover Lamb—in the event that we should use our free will to rebel against God. The rituals of the Old Testament sanctuary also made it obvious: the angels knew *why* Christ came as a babe in Bethlehem. He *wanted* to give His life for us.

It couldn't have been easy for angels to hold their peace while we heaped disgrace and shame on God's perfect Son. I am sure it was all they could do to hold themselves back. If Jesus had just given the word, they would have sprung into action and put an end to the horrible spectacle of the cross—but the word never came. Jesus *wanted* to be your Passover.

When Jesus was first arrested, Peter pulled out his sword to defend Him. Jesus told him to put it away.

"Listen, Peter," He said, "don't you think I could call 12 legions of angels if I really wanted to?[60]

Don't you think I could put a stop to this?" Jesus wasn't a helpless martyr. He didn't go to the cross because He had no choice. He suffered and died deliberately because it was the only way *you* could be spared from the wages of sin.

Don't get me wrong—Jesus didn't *want* to suffer. He didn't enjoy pain any more than you do. In the Garden of Gethsemane, the suffering became so terrible that Jesus actually asked His Father to remove it from Him:

He went a little farther and fell on His face, and prayed, saying, "O My Father, if it is possible, let this cup pass from Me; nevertheless, not as I will, but as You will." (Matthew 26:39)

Jesus didn't go to the cross because He had no choice; He went to the cross because *you* were out of options. He went because it was the will of the Father to save you. The nails didn't hold God's Son to the cross; He was held there by His desire to see you stand in the presence of God:

"...looking unto Jesus, the author and finisher of our faith, who for the joy that was set before Him endured the cross, despising the shame, and has sat down at the right hand of the throne of God." (Heb. 12:2)

What was the "joy that was set before Him?" I am convinced that it has something to do with the knowledge that you could one day find yourself forever in His presence because of the gift of the cross.

The angels didn't stop the crucifixion, but try to imagine how hard it must have been for them to watch it. Then try to comprehend the disbelief in heaven when somebody rejects Christ's gift.

There is a famous story in circulation about a man who operated a lift bridge for passenger trains. One day, he took his little son to work, and as the day wore on he lost track of where his son was playing. He looked all over for his boy. To his horror, he discovered that he had fallen into the gearbox that raised and lowered the bridge. It was at that very moment that he heard a train approaching.

What was he going to do? A whole train full of people would plunge into the river if he didn't lower the bridge—but if he lowered it, his only son would be crushed to death. There wasn't much time to deliberate. He knew what he had to do. He couldn't sacrifice everyone else's loved ones to save his own. So he ran back to the hut, closed his eyes, and lowered the bridge. The train was safe. His son was lost.

As he watched the train pass by, he noticed through the tears in his eyes that the people inside had no idea they had just been saved. They were talking and laughing with each other, or engrossed in magazines and books. Nobody—absolutely nobody—noticed the little boy whose life had just been sacrificed to save them.

It was more than the father could bear, and even though his voice was drowned out by the thunder of the train, he screamed out in agony.

"Don't you care?" he shrieked. "Don't you care that I just gave up my only son to save you?"

There is a passage in the book of Hebrews that speaks volumes about what happens when we deliberately turn our backs on God:

For it is impossible for those who were once enlightened, and have tasted the heavenly gift, and have become partakers of the Holy Spirit, and have tasted the good word of God and the powers of the age to come, if they fall away, to renew them again to repentance, since they crucify again for themselves the Son of God, and put Him to an open shame. (Hebrews 6:4-6)

Elsewhere, the Bible is clear that Jesus died *once* to save us. That was enough to redeem us from our sins. Yet here it says that Jesus is crucified *again*. How can that be? When we deliberately choose to go on sinning, it's like crucifying Jesus all over again. We refuse the gift and put Him back on the cross. As angels watch in absolute disbelief, we walk away from the cross of Calvary and refuse to accept it. It's as if you are a passenger on a recently saved train, indifferent to the fact that your safety cost Him *everything*.

The lessons of the Passover are clear. You have a Passover Lamb, and without Him, you must face the plague of death yourself. But He is not going to force the issue. Like the Passover lamb of old, you are invited to examine Him to see if He really is everything He claims to be, and then it's up to you: will you sprinkle the blood of God's Son on the doorposts of your heart?

---

[49] *Sheol* is a Hebrew word that refers to the grave.
[50] John 12
[51] Luke 19
[52] John 18:19-21
[53] F. C. Gilbert, *Practical Lessons*, p. 238, 239.
[54] John 1:29, 36
[55] 1 Corinthians 5:7
[56] 1 Peter 1:18, 19
[57] Revelation 5:6
[58] John 15:13
[59] Martha Zimmerman, *Celebrate the Feasts of the Old Testament*, np.
[60] Matthew 26:53

CHAPTER TEN

The Last Enemy

In 1985, Robert Funk called the first meeting of the *Jesus Seminar*, a group of renegade Bible scholars whose self-appointed task is to call the authenticity of the Biblical account of the life of Jesus into question. They meet twice a year to vote on which parts of the four gospels they will accept as true, and which parts they refuse to believe.

In 1995, they gathered to vote on what *Time* magazine called the "most explosive question of the Christian faith." *Did Jesus literally rise from the dead?* An overwhelming majority of those in attendance voted that He did not. That decision understandably caused outrage in the Christian community. How could so-called Christians deny the one event that *defines* the Christian faith?

The *Jesus Seminar* is not the first group to deny the resurrection of Jesus. Some years ago, for example, author Hugh J. Schonfield, wrote a book called *The Passover Plot*. In it, he described the resurrection as an elaborate conspiracy devised by Jesus and a secret group of His followers from Jerusalem.

Because Jesus knew Himself to be a descendant of David, Schonfield argued that He deliberately made the events in His life correspond to Messianic prophecies, and that the culmination of His master plan was to stage a resurrection from the dead to convince others to accept His leadership.

One of the biggest problems with *The Passover Plot* is that it has Jesus scheming to deceive the world into thinking He is the Messiah, when not a scrap of biblical evidence even begins to suggest such a thing. The resurrection was supposed to be a fake; Jesus would be rescued from the cross, and then reported as risen from the dead. According to Schonfield, however, the plan went horribly wrong when a Roman soldier thrust his spear into Jesus' side. The "conspirators" were then forced to make His body disappear to an unmarked grave. The result? An empty tomb, and a group of disciples—not privy to the plot—mistakenly believing in a resurrection.

Schonfield was not the first to weave a tale like this—not by a long shot. Notice what the Bible says happened when the guards who had been posted at Jesus' tomb came to inform the priests that Jesus was no longer dead:

Now while they were going, behold, some of the guard came into the city and reported to the chief priests all the things that had happened. When they had assembled with the elders and consulted together, they gave a large sum of money to the soldiers, saying, "Tell them, 'His disciples came at night and stole Him away while we slept.' And if this comes to the governor's ears, we will appease him and make you secure." (Matthew 28:11-14)

Schonfield got it wrong: oh yes, there *was* a plot to cover up what had happened, but Jesus' supporters didn't hatch it. His enemies developed it in a desperate attempt to hide the fact that they had been wrong about Jesus, and that the resurrection had actually taken place. They must have offered the soldiers a *lot* of money to lie, because no Roman soldier would freely admit that he had fallen asleep on the job. Sleeping on duty was punishable by death.

Ever since the chief priests hatched the first lie about the resurrection of Christ, there have been other people eagerly following in their footsteps, trying to disprove it.

If they really understood what took place at the cross, and why the resurrection is so important, they wouldn't be in such a hurry to dismiss it. If Christ didn't rise from the dead, we have a huge problem on our hands.

The Apostle Paul wrote that if Jesus Christ did not literally rise from the dead, we have no basis whatsoever for Christianity. Without a living

Savior, there is no hope. Without the literal, bodily resurrection of Christ, we would still be lost in our sins—and death would simply be the end:

And if Christ is not risen, your faith is futile; you are still in your sins! Then also those who have fallen asleep in Christ have perished. If in this life only we have hope in Christ, we are of all men the most pitiable. (1 Corinthians 15:17-19)

Instinctively, many people realize that if God does not exist and the Bible is not true, we don't have much hope. When George H. Bush was Vice President of the United States, he was chosen to represent his country at the funeral of Leonid Brezhnev. The funeral was much like any other Soviet state funeral, except for something peculiar he noticed happening near the end of the ceremony. As the soldiers reached for the coffin lid to close it for the last time, Brezhnev's widow suddenly stretched out her arm and traced a cross over the chest of her dead husband. The Soviet Union was an atheistic empire; they did not officially believe in the death and resurrection of Christ. At that moment, Mrs. Brezhnev desperately hoped they were wrong.

The rituals of the ancient tabernacle clearly foreshadowed Christ's triumphant return from the grave. On the third day of the Passover week, the Israelites celebrated the Feast of Firstfruits:

And the LORD spoke to Moses, saying, "Speak to the children of Israel, and say to them: 'When you come into the land which I give to you, and reap its harvest, then you shall bring a sheaf of the firstfruits of your harvest to the priest. He shall wave the sheaf before the LORD, to be accepted on your behalf; on the day after the Sabbath the priest shall wave it.'" (Leviticus 23:9-11)

Passover occurred in the month of Nisan,[61] when the barley was ripening in the fields. It was celebrated on the fourteenth day, and on that day a certain section of the barley field was set aside for the upcoming Feast of Firstfruits. Sheaves of barley from this section were tied together and then cut. On the sixteenth the priest took a sheaf of barley and "waved it" before the Lord.

This was a deeply meaningful event. That one sheaf of barley pointed forward to a great harvest, and it was presented to God as a way of thanking Him for the crop to come. The ceremony took place on the *third day* of the Passover, which marks the moment when Jesus rose from the grave—on the third day after His death!

Jesus was crucified on the fourteenth of the month, on the very day that the priests were prepared to offer the Passover lamb in the temple. He was laid to rest in the tomb and stayed there over the Sabbath hours. Early on the morning of the sixteenth, the women went to the grave to finish embalming His body, but He wasn't there!

The resurrection of Christ took place on the very day that the priest took the firstfruits of the barley harvest and presented it to God. This is why Paul describes Jesus as the "firstfruits":

But now Christ is risen from the dead, and has become the firstfruits of those who have fallen asleep. (1 Corinthians 15:20)

The "wave sheaf" offering was a demonstration of faith that the rest of the harvest would follow. When Jesus conquered the grave, He did it for *us*. He became the "firstfruits of those who have fallen asleep." The resurrection of Christ is proof that God knows how to conquer the grave. We can have faith that since Jesus has come back from the dead, many others will also one day come back:

But each one in his own order: Christ the firstfruits, afterward those who are Christ's at His coming. (1 Corinthians 15:23)

Christ's resurrection is God's pledge that we will not suffer the consequences of sin forever. In the end, when the Holy City descends to earth, death will be destroyed, and we will have everlasting life in the presence of God.

The catacombs of Rome are a series of underground tunnels and crypts that served as an ancient graveyard. They extend for hundreds of miles under the ground, and the walls of the tunnels are pockmarked with thousands of small shelves and openings just big enough to hold a human body. The early Christians were among those who buried their dead in the catacombs, believing that when Jesus returned, the dead would live again.

The walls of the catacombs are periodically marked with inscriptions and symbols, left there by early believers. In some places, you will find pictures of the Good Shepherd, a well-loved symbol for Jesus. In other places, you will find a fish engraved in the soft stone, which was an early symbol for Christ (the Latin word for fish was an acrostic for the phrase *Jesus Christ, Son of God, Savior*).

Some of the most interesting marks, however, are those left above the graves of loved ones. There is a distinct difference between the inscriptions written over the graves of Christians and those written over the graves of non-believers.

Some graves have hopeless phrases like *goodbye for all eternity* inscribed on them, as if the families of those who died never expected to see them again. The graves of Christians, however, are different. They are not hopeless. They say things like *goodbye until we meet again,* or *goodbye until the morning.* Early Christians knew something that others did not: Christ has conquered death. The firstfruits of the resurrection have already been presented to God; He is their great High Priest in heaven, and the great harvest will shortly come to pass.

This is why the Second Coming is often referred to in the language of harvest in the Bible, as in these passages:

Then I looked, and behold, a white cloud, and on the cloud sat One like the Son of Man, having on His head a golden crown, and in His hand a sharp sickle. And another angel came out of the temple, crying with a loud voice to Him who sat on the cloud, "Thrust in Your sickle and reap, for the time has come for You to reap, for the harvest of the earth is ripe." So He who sat on the cloud thrust in His sickle on the earth, and the earth was reaped.[62] *(Revelation 14:14-16)*

...His disciples came to Him, saying, "Explain to us the parable of the tares of the field." He answered and said to them: "He who sows the good seed is the Son of Man. The field is the world, the good seeds are the sons of the kingdom, but the tares are the sons of the wicked one. The enemy who sowed them is the devil, the harvest is the end of the age, and the reapers are the angels." (Matthew 13:36b-39)

The hope of Christianity is the empty tomb of Christ. He rose from the dead with a real, physical body. He invited His disciples to touch Him and then He ate food in front of them. He conquered death, and because of that, we will also be resurrected from the dead:

But I do not want you to be ignorant, brethren, concerning those who have fallen asleep, lest you sorrow as others who have no hope. For if we believe that Jesus died and rose again, even so God will bring with Him those who sleep in Jesus. (1 Thessalonians 4:13, 14)

What is Paul saying? Because we know that Jesus rose from the dead, we can have confidence that those who have fallen asleep (died) in Christ will also come out of their graves and return to heaven with Him. He continues:

For the Lord Himself will descend from heaven with a shout, with the voice of an archangel, and with the trumpet of God. And the dead in Christ will rise first. Then we who are alive and remain shall be caught up together with them in the clouds to meet the Lord in the air. And thus we shall always be with the Lord. Therefore comfort one another with these words. (1 Thessalonians 4:16-18)

On that morning, widows will have their husbands back. Orphans will have their parents back. Grieving mothers will finally blink away their tears as they are reunited with children that have been lost to the cruel grasp of the grave. From that moment on, we will dwell in the presence of Jesus forever in a place where there is no more death.[63]

There is coming a day when the last funeral will have been conducted and the last tear will have been shed. When the trumpet sounds, those things will be finished. The Bible calls death our enemy.[64] On that day, our enemy will have been destroyed.

Today, when you die, you can have your body (or just your head) cryogenically frozen so that when medical science finds a cure for what killed you, they can thaw you out and bring you back to life. Some have spent small fortunes on this process, hoping it will bring them immortality. There's even a persistent rumor circulating that Walt Disney's body was preserved this way (all evidence indicates, however, that this is a well-circulated urban legend).

Why do people do it? They want to cheat the Grim Reaper—but to date, nobody has ever succeeded. We may be able to extend our lifespan by a few years, but we have utterly failed to overcome death itself. And yet there is hope. Jesus holds the keys of death:

"I am He who lives, and was dead, and behold, I am alive forevermore. Amen. And I have the keys of Hades and of Death." (Revelation 1:18)

The firstfruits have already been presented to God. You can be certain that the rest of the harvest will come, too. You don't have to die without hope.

A man and his wife were driving one snowy day when the weather suddenly took a turn for the worse, and they found themselves trapped in a blizzard. Before long, the storm became so bad that they could no longer drive. Stranded, they were forced to wait the storm out.

The blizzard persisted much longer than they could have anticipated, dumping masses of snow all around their vehicle. Escape now became completely impossible; they were buried alive. The next day, rescue workers found their frozen bodies inside the car. As they were lifting the woman out of her seat, they noticed something hanging out of the glove compartment. It was a note she had scribbled before she died: *I don't want to die this way.*

The real tragedy was that there was a bus that was also stranded just a few feet away from their icy grave. Its passengers were warm and comfortable throughout the night. In fact, they thought it was fun to be stranded, and made it a festive occasion. The snow had been so heavy that the ill-fated couple couldn't see the bus. They died just a few feet from salvation!

Far too many people reach the end of life and are forced to say, "I don't want to die this way!" They are alone, without hope. That is a tragedy, because hope is closer than they might imagine. What is your hope? Is the grave the end for you—or have you noticed that your Heavenly Wave Sheaf Offering has already secured a place for you in the presence of God?

---

[61] Before the Babylonian captivity, *Nisan* was commonly called *Abib.*
[62] It's also interesting to note the reference to the temple in this passage.
[63] Revelation 21:4
[64] 1 Corinthians 15:26

CHAPTER ELEVEN

Tongues of Fire

Jerusalem had suddenly become a very busy place. There were Jews visiting from all across the Roman Empire for the feast of Pentecost. Those who believed that Jesus was the Messiah were all gathered together in one place, when suddenly there was a loud noise, and tongues of fire began to dance above each head. They started to speak in languages they had never studied or spoken before.

The visitors were absolutely amazed. No matter where they were visiting from, they could hear the story of Jesus in their own language:

Then they were all amazed and marveled, saying to one another, "Look, are not all these who speak Galileans? And how is it that we hear, each in our own language in which we were born? Parthians and Medes and Elamites, those dwelling in Mesopotamia, Judea and Cappadocia, Pontus and Asia, Phrygia and Pamphylia, Egypt and the parts of Libya adjoining Cyrene, visitors from Rome, both Jews and proselytes, Cretans and Arabs–we hear them speaking in our own tongues the wonderful works of God." (Acts 2:7-11)

Naturally, everyone was excited, but this divine reversal of Babel was only the tip of the iceberg because it happened to coincide with the Feast of Pentecost.

Of course, this was not an accident. Pentecost fell on the fiftieth day after the Passover, and like the Feast of Firstfruits, it was also a harvest festival, where the firstfruits of the entire spring harvest were celebrated:

And you shall count for yourselves from the day after the Sabbath, from the day that you brought the sheaf of the wave offering: seven Sabbaths shall be completed. Count fifty days to the day after the seventh Sabbath; then you shall offer a new grain offering to the LORD. You shall bring from your dwellings two wave loaves of two-tenths of an ephah. They shall be of fine flour; they shall be baked with leaven. They are the firstfruits to the LORD. And you shall offer with the bread seven lambs of the first year, without blemish, one young bull, and two rams. They shall be as a burnt offering to the LORD, with their grain offering and their drink offerings, an offering made by fire for a sweet aroma to the LORD. Then you shall sacrifice one kid of the goats as a sin offering, and two male lambs of the first year as a sacrifice of a peace offering. The priest shall wave them with the bread of the firstfruits as a wave offering before the LORD, with the two lambs. They shall be holy to the LORD for the priest. (Leviticus 23:15-20)

Jesus remained on earth for 40 days after the resurrection before He returned to heaven. Prior to leaving, He instructed His disciples to wait in Jerusalem until they received the gift of the Holy Spirit, which would give them the power to carry the gospel to the world. Jesus said that it would happen "not many days from now."[65] The waiting period turned out to be only 10 days.

As tongues of Holy fire danced above each head, the disciples were filled with unusual power to carry the gospel message to the world. Even though the physical presence of Christ had been removed from the earth, He was still with them in the Person of the Holy Spirit.

"There are difficult days ahead," He had warned the disciples. "I am returning to my Father in heaven, and the world will turn against you for sharing what I have taught you. Ironically, they will think they are actually doing God a favor by persecuting you. It's not going to be an easy existence, so I am sending you some Help."[66]

What was the purpose of the Holy Spirit? Jesus lays it out clearly in the sixteenth and seventeenth chapters of John's gospel. Jesus had a plan to perpetuate the presence of God among His people. The Holy Spirit would be given to the church to sustain their personal contact with Christ. At the same time, He would embolden and empower them to share Christ's teachings with the world. This would create a state of affairs in which the presence of God would be manifested to the world through the work of the church:

"But when the Helper comes, whom I shall send to you from the Father, the Spirit of truth who proceeds from the Father, He will testify of Me. And you also will bear witness, because you have been with Me from the beginning." (John 15:26, 27)

In addition to maintaining a living link between Christ and the church and mobilizing God's people for active duty, the Holy Spirit—the third member of the Godhead, also performs a number of other critical functions:

1. He serves to activate the conscience. In John 16:8-11, Jesus instructs His disciples that one of the roles of the Holy Spirit is to "convict the world of sin, and of righteousness, and of judgment." He enables us to feel remorse for sin, and He brings conviction to the heart.

2. He keeps us in contact with Christ. In John 16:12-14 Jesus tells us that the Holy Spirit will be the vehicle through which Christ continues to teach His church. The Spirit (a) guides us into truth, relaying the teachings of Christ to us (b) shows us things to come, and (c) glorifies Christ.[67]

3. He enables and empowers the church to carry out the task entrusted to it by Jesus. Paul informs us in 1 Corinthians 12 that the Spirit gives individual believers certain gifts so that they can function as a part of the organized work of the church as a whole. The Holy Spirit chooses who receives which gifts, acting as a sort of Master Coordinator for the work of spreading the gospel.

There is a grave misunderstanding in some corners of Christianity about the "gifts of the Spirit." These gifts were given to us for the purpose of active service in reaching the world for Christ. They were given "for the equipping of the saints for the work of ministry."[68] Yet in some parts of Christendom, spiritual gifts appear to have become something of a sideshow for the saints, where the gifts themselves have become more important than the function they were intended to perform. Miraculous manifestations have become "proof" that God is with us personally. That is a dangerous approach, because in the last days of earth's history, miracles will begin to occur in all the wrong places:

And I saw three unclean spirits like frogs coming out of the mouth of the dragon, out of the mouth of the beast, and out of the mouth of the false prophet. For they are spirits of demons, performing signs, which go out to the kings of the earth and of the whole world, to gather them to the battle of that great day of God Almighty. (Revelation 16:13, 14)

He performs great signs, so that he even makes fire come down from heaven on the earth in the sight of men. And he deceives those who dwell on the earth by those signs which he was granted to do in the sight of the beast, telling those who dwell on the earth to make an image to the beast who was wounded by the sword and lived. (Revelation 13:13, 14)

Miracles are not *proof* of God's Presence. There is no question in my mind that God continues to work miracles today; I have been witness to many of them. Yet when God's people begin to emphasize "signs and wonders" rather than the work God has given us to do, I fear that we are setting ourselves up to become victims of an overpowering last-day deception.

Furthermore, in recent years, some Christians have begun to insist that everyone must receive the same miraculous "gift" as proof that their spiritual experience is real. There are a number of problems with this concept. First of all, the Bible is clear that all Christians do *not* receive the same gift. This is abundantly clear in passages like 1 Corinthians 12, where Paul reminds us that we are all differently gifted so that we can perform different functions in the body of Christ, the church. If everyone were given the same gift, it would paralyze the church in the work of spreading the gospel.

Our unity as Christians is based on the fact that we *must* work together because individual Christians are not able to carry out Christ's commission on their own. Secondly, it is important to remember that spiritual gifts were *not* given as entertainment for believers. The Spirit of God specifically assigns our spiritual gifts to us so that we can function powerfully—in an organized fashion—to quickly bring the gospel to the whole world.[69]

The gift of the Spirit was poured out on the church at a significant moment in the religious calendar of Israel. Pentecost was not only a harvest celebration (notice, by the way, that the first large "harvest" of the church took place on this day, with 3,000 people accepting the message and joining the church); it was also considered the anniversary of Israel's gathering at Mount Sinai 50 days after their exodus from Egypt. It was at Mount Sinai that the Israelites encountered the presence of God in a dramatic way, and where they received a hand written copy of His Ten Commandments. Moses had met Him in a burning bush; the Israelites saw Him in a burning mountain:

Then it came to pass on the third day, in the morning, that there were thunderings and lightnings, and a thick cloud on the mountain; and the sound of the trumpet was very loud, so that all the people who were in the camp trembled. And Moses brought the people out of the camp to meet with God, and they stood at the foot of the mountain. Now Mount Sinai was completely in smoke, because the LORD descended upon it in fire. Its smoke ascended like the smoke of a furnace, and the whole mountain quaked greatly. And when the blast of the trumpet sounded long and became louder and louder, Moses spoke, and God answered him by voice. (Exodus 19:16-19)

There is a direct link between the New Testament Day of Pentecost and the giving of God's law at Mount Sinai. Jerome, the man who translated the scriptures into Latin during the fourth century, noticed this distinct connection:

There is Sinai; here is Sion; there the trembling mountain, here the trembling house; there the flaming mountain, here the flaming tongues; there the noisy thunderings, here the sounds of many tongues; there the clangor of the ram's horn, here the notes of the gospel trumpet.[70]

John Keble, the famous poet and Oxford scholar, also noticed the direct relationship between the events at mount Sinai and the New Testament day of Pentecost:

When God of old came down from heaven,
In power and wrath He came;
Before His feet the clouds were riven,
Half darkness and half flame:

The fires, that rushed on Sinai down,
In sudden torrents dread,

Now gently light, a glorious crown,
On every sainted head.

And as on Israel's awestruck ear
The voice exceeding loud,
The trump that angels quake to hear
Thrilled from the deep, dark cloud;

So, when the Spirit of our God
Came down His flock to find,
A voice from heaven was heard abroad,
A rushing, mighty wind.[71]

At the moment the ancient Israelites were led out of Egyptian captivity and commissioned by God to claim the Promised Land as their own, He visited them in a dramatic way. The same thing happened in the New Testament. Christians, having recently been liberated from the slavery of sin by the cross of Christ, were told to go to the whole world and claim the hearts of humanity for Christ. God sent them off to win the world with a dramatic manifestation of His presence in the Holy Spirit.

Now the Ten Commandments were no longer just written on tables of stone; they were written in the hearts of Christ's followers.[72] These followers became consumed with the idea of bringing Christ to the world. They—as a collective whole, and through the presence and power of the Holy Spirit—became the presence of God on earth.

As exciting as Pentecost was for the disciples, what took place on earth that day was only the tip of the iceberg. If you read the second chapter of Acts carefully, you will notice an unusual statement made by Peter, indicating that the *real* action was taking place in heaven:

"This Jesus God has raised up, of which we are all witnesses. Therefore being exalted to the right hand of God, and having received from the Father the promise of the Holy Spirit, He poured out this which you now see and hear." (Acts 2:32, 33)

The old King James Version tells us that Jesus "shed forth" the Holy Spirit. The primary event that takes place at Pentecost was not on earth; it was in heaven. The primary focus was not the church; it was Jesus Christ. The Holy Spirit was given to Christ, and then He gave it to us.

It was as if the Spirit was poured over Him, spilling onto the church below.

Peter's statement takes on deeper meaning when you study the Old Testament sanctuary. When the High Priest was consecrated for service, part of the ritual included anointing him with oil:

"Then you shall take the garments, put the tunic on Aaron, and the robe of the ephod, the ephod, and the breastplate, and gird him with the intricately woven band of the ephod. You shall put the turban on his head, and put the holy crown on the turban. And you shall take the anointing oil, pour it on his head, and anoint him." (Exodus 29:5-7)

Peter is saying that when Christ went back to heaven He received the "promise of the Holy Spirit." He was anointed as the High Priest in Heaven's sanctuary. His death and resurrection had brought an end to the earthly sacrificial system, and now the ministry in *heaven's* sanctuary had begun. Like the earthly sanctuary, heaven's sanctuary has a High Priest, and like the earthly High Priest, He was anointed—not with oil, but with the Holy Spirit.

There is an interesting passage found in the book of Psalms that ties together the anointing of the High Priest with the perfect unity found among the disciples on the day of Pentecost:

Behold, how good and how pleasant it is for brethren to dwell together in unity! It is like the precious oil upon the head, running down on the beard, the beard of Aaron, running down on the edge of his garments. (Psalm 133:1, 2)

When you read this Psalm through the eyes of Pentecost, it speaks volumes. There is a direct link between Christian unity and the anointing of the High Priest. The book of Acts tells us that when the Holy Spirit was poured out on the fledgling New Testament church, "they were all with one accord in one place."[73] Then Peter tells an amazed crowd that the Holy Spirit had been given to Jesus and then passed on to the church. There is a point to be made here that should not be missed: Christian unity comes as the result of the Spirit's mobilization of the church for active witness. We do not find unity in debating the finer points of theology. We do not find unity by simply praying for it. We find perfect unity when we are activated by God's Spirit for service.

On the day of Pentecost, Jesus was anointed as our great High Priest. His sacrifice in the courtyard (the earth) was sufficient for our sins. He had earned the right to represent the fallen human race before the throne of God. Many Bible scholars see a description of Christ's inauguration as heaven's High Priest in the events portrayed in the fifth chapter of Revelation:

Then I looked, and I heard the voice of many angels around the throne, the living creatures, and the elders; and the number of them was ten thousand times ten thousand, and thousands of thousands, saying with a loud voice: "Worthy is the Lamb who was slain to receive power and riches and wisdom, and strength and honor and glory and blessing!" And every creature which is in heaven and on the earth and under the earth and such as are in the sea, and all that are in them, I heard saying: "Blessing and honor and glory and power be to Him who sits on the throne, and to the Lamb, forever and ever!" Then the four living creatures said, "Amen!" And the twenty-four elders fell down and worshiped Him who lives forever and ever. (Revelation 5:11-14)

The tongues of fire on earth were only a small representation of a celebration that was taking place in heaven. It was a dual anointing: the day that Christ began His ministry in heaven's sanctuary was the day that His followers were also anointed as a "royal priesthood" on earth.[74] The church, imbued with the power of the Holy Spirit, was given the ministry of reconciling sinners to the Savior.[75]

The day of Pentecost signaled the beginning of a partnership in which Jesus has commissioned us to be voices for heaven. Others can experience the presence of God through us. And when the gospel has finally been preached in "all the world," Jesus will lay aside His priestly robes in heaven, and come back for us.

---

[65] Acts 1:5

[66] See John 16:1-7 for a complete account of Jesus' instruction.

[67] See also John 15:26, where Jesus says that the Spirit will testify of Him.

[68] Ephesians 4:12

[69] A good example is the gift of tongues, which has become one of the most misunderstood gifts in the Christian church. 1 Corinthians 14:22 tells us specifically that tongues are a sign for *unbelievers*, not believers. And yet it is often used in some Christian churches as evidence for believers that God is present among them. If you study the gift of tongues carefully in the Bible, you'll notice that it is only manifested when foreigners are present–people who need to hear the gospel. And in the only explanation of this gift presented in the Bible, it is understood to be the miraculous ability to communicate in *real* languages.

[70] Bacchiocci, vol 1, p. 188   [71] Ibid., p. 187

[72] Hebrews 10:16, 17   [73] Acts 2:1   [74] 1 Peter 2:9   [75] 2 Corinthians 5:17-20

CHAPTER TWELVE

Early Warning

At the time of its construction, the WAC Bennett Dam in Canada was the largest earth-filled dam in the world. It was made from 57 million cubic yards of fill—enough to build a wall nine feet high and twelve feet wide all the way from Vancouver, British Columbia to Halifax, Nova Scotia![76] The cost—an absolute fortune in that day—was $750 million. When you stand on top of the dam and look down into the valley beneath it, the view nearly takes your breath away. It is a *very* big dam.

What is even more impressive, however, is the body of water created when workers constructed the dam back in the 1960s. The majestic Peace River was backed up behind the structure, creating the largest lake in the province of British Columbia. Williston Lake also happens to be one of the largest man-made lakes in the world: it is 225 kilometers long with a surface area of more than 437,000 acres. There is a lot of water behind the dam!

On June 15, 1996, some tourists were driving the mile-and-a-quarter stretch across the top of the dam when they noticed a hole in the pavement. Instinctively, they knew that holes in a dam are not a good thing, so they mentioned their discovery to workers at the generating station. Engineers examined the perforation in the pavement and discovered a serious sinkhole. Further investigation uncovered a second one. Was the dam's integrity compromised?

Word of the potential problem quickly spread to Hudson's Hope, a little community of about a thousand people situated several miles downstream from the dam. As you can imagine, the community had cause for concern. If the dam breached, what would happen to their town? Some people estimated that Hudson's Hope would be buried under 400 feet of water for almost a week should the structure become compromised.

The dam's spillway was opened to lower the level of the lake, enabling crews to begin repairs. Merely opening the spillway caused the Peace River to rise by more than six feet, flooding the properties along the river. When the lake had been lowered to more than 50 feet below its maximum level, teams began drilling and repairing the sinkholes.

The unimaginable did not happen; the dam was repaired and the town of Hudson's Hope is now safer than ever. The possibility of a breach, however, will be there as long as the dam exists. Just in case something *does* happen one day, the town is equipped with an early warning system—seven large air horns scattered throughout the community. If the dam breaks the horns will be sounded, notifying residents that a wall of water is bearing down on the town and they have only minutes to head for higher ground.

While visiting Hudson's Hope one evening, I heard the mournful wail of the early warning system. I was at a meeting in the local hotel, and when the sirens began blaring, I instinctively reached for my car keys so I could make a quick escape. (This happened not long after the sinkholes were discovered.) Nobody else moved. What I didn't realize at the time was that they tested the system once a week to make sure it worked!

That night, as I drove home, I did a lot of thinking. If the emergency had been real, would I be faced with regrets over the things in life that I did not accomplish? At some point in life we come to the place where we realize that we only have a little time left to live. In your imagination, try to place yourself in the community of Hudson's Hope for a moment. The sirens are wailing, and people are scrambling to jump into their cars. There are only 15 minutes left before the waters from Williston Lake engulf the town.

What would you do with your 15 minutes? What is a priority when you are out of time? Would you rush home to grab the tape out of your VCR because you couldn't bear to miss a single episode of *The Apprentice*? Would you scramble to find a crowbar so you could pry open your safety deposit box? Would you waste your time trying to load the trunk of your car with possessions?

The passengers of the Titanic were forced to answer that question. Nobody expected the end to come so quickly. Major A. H. Peuchens was on board that night and managed to survive. When he realized that the ship was quickly slipping into the icy waters of the North Atlantic, he ran to his cabin where he had more than $300,000 worth of valuables locked in a strongbox. He ran past the box and grabbed three oranges, since they seemed more valuable to him at that moment, because money can't keep you alive in a rowboat.

Let's take this matter a little further. What if heaven had an early warning system? What if one day, you suddenly heard a siren sounding, letting you know that the judgment hour was about to begin?

The annual festivals of the ancient Israelites had an early warning system built into them that let the people know when their *annual* day of judgment was approaching. Much like the air horns over Hudson's Hope, trumpets were sounded in the camp to warn that time was growing short:

Then the LORD spoke to Moses, saying, "Speak to the children of Israel, saying: 'In the seventh month, on the first day of the month, you shall have a sabbath-rest, a memorial of blowing of trumpets, a holy convocation.'" (Leviticus 23:23, 24)

Trumpets were blown on the first day of the seventh month, which was actually the first day of the year. How can the first day of the year be in the seventh month? Israel had two calendars—a civil calendar and a religious calendar. The religious calendar began with the Passover in the spring, and the civil calendar began with the blowing of the trumpets on the first day of the seventh month. That's why, even though the Feast of Trumpets takes place in the seventh month, it is known as Rosh Hashanah, the Jewish New Year. It is the beginning of the *civil* year.

Why blow trumpets? It was a clear warning:

Also the tenth day of this seventh month shall be the Day of Atonement. It shall be a holy convocation for you; you shall afflict your souls, and offer an offering made by fire to the LORD. And you shall do no work on that same day, for it is the Day of Atonement, to make atonement for you before the LORD your God. For any person who is not afflicted in soul on that same day shall be cut off from his people. (Leviticus 23:27-29)

The sounding of the trumpets delivered a clear warning that the Day of Atonement was rapidly approaching. Time was quickly running out. F. C. Gilbert, a former Jew and Christian author, describes the blowing of trumpets like this:

The Talmud teaches that the blowing of the trumpets signifies God's loud call to repentance. Since this seventh month closes up the year's work in connection with the sanctuary service, and with the harvest, how appropriate for the trumpet to blow, that the people should turn their attention more to the things of God, and prepare for the final work. Hence this is made one of the most sacred days to the Jews. They also teach that on this day three sets of books are opened–the book of life to examine the good deeds of the people, the book of death to examine the evil deeds, and a sort of intermediary book to examine into the accounts of those whose cases are to be decided at the Day of Atonement, ten days later. The ten days following this sabbath day are called, "The ten days of repentance." The most careless and indifferent during these days devotes his time to the service of God, and seeks for preparation of heart that when the Day of Atonement arrives he may receive a "seal" of life for the year to come.[77]

The blowing of trumpets was a wake-up call. It underscored the fact that the judgment hour was quickly approaching, when it would be determined who was still a part of Israel and who was not.

All year long sin was symbolically transferred from penitent sinners to sacrificial animals, and then the sacrificial blood was carried into the tabernacle. This symbolic "transfer of sin" created a problem, because the sanctuary was God's dwelling, and sin was defiling it. Once a year, on the Day of Atonement (also known as Yom Kippur), a ritual was performed that cleansed the sanctuary of all the sins that had been symbolically transferred into it:

"So he shall make atonement for the Holy Place, because of the uncleanness of the children of Israel, and because of their transgressions, for all their sins; and so he shall do for the tabernacle of meeting which remains among them in the midst of their uncleanness." (Lev. 16:16)

This was the only day of the year in which the High Priest could enter the Most Holy Place of the tabernacle. According to the sixteenth chapter of Leviticus, two goats were brought to the tabernacle, and by means of drawing lots, one of the goats was chosen "for the Lord," and the other one was designated as a "scapegoat."[78] The "Lord's goat" was offered as a sin offering, after which the High Priest would take its blood into the Most Holy Place and sprinkle it on the mercy seat.[79] This way, the "uncleanness of the children of Israel" was removed from the sanctuary. What happens next is absolutely fascinating:

"And when he has made an end of atoning for the Holy Place, the tabernacle of meeting, and the altar, he shall bring the live goat. Aaron shall lay both his hands on the head of the live goat, confess over it all the iniquities of the children of Israel, and all their transgressions, concerning all their sins, putting them on the head of the goat, and shall send it away into the wilderness by the hand of a suitable man. The goat shall bear on itself all their iniquities to an uninhabited land; and he shall release the goat in the wilderness." (Leviticus 16:20-22)

After the sanctuary was cleansed, the High Priest moved back outside and placed his hands on the head of the live goat. The sins that had been cleansed from the sanctuary were transferred to the scapegoat, and then it was driven out into the wilderness—banished forever. The meaning of the first goat is clear; it was slain for sin, pointing us to the blood of Christ. The second goat, however, was *not* slain. It was banished.

What does the second goat represent? I have read many books that suggest that the second goat also represents Christ because of the sins that are heaped on it. While it is an understandable conclusion, there are a couple of problems with this understanding:

(1) **The scapegoat is never slain.** It is not sacrificed, and its blood is used nowhere in the sanctuary service. In describing the rituals of the sanctuary and how they represent the work of Christ, Hebrews 9:22 reminds us that "without shedding of blood is no remission." The scapegoat is not a *substitutionary* animal; it does not take anyone's place. The "Lord's goat" has already served as a sacrificial substitute.

(2) **The scapegoat has an unusual name.** When you read Leviticus 16:8 in the original language, it tells us that the first goat was "for the Lord," and the second goat was "for *Azazel*."[80] Who or what is Azazel? Throw that word into a search engine like Google and its chilling meaning

will surface quickly because of the number of occult practitioners who pay reverence to him. Azazel is a *demonic* figure. Note this explanation in the *Jewish Encyclopedia:*

The name of a supernatural being mentioned in connection with the ritual of the Day of Atonement (Lev. xvi.). After Satan, for whom he was in some degree a preparation, **Azazel** *enjoys the distinction of being the most mysterious extrahuman character in sacred literature. Unlike other Hebrew proper names, the name itself is obscure.*[81]

Leslie Hardinge, in his masterful work on the sanctuary, points out why the scapegoat cannot possibly represent Jesus Christ:

*Since Yahweh is a personal name for the Deity, many Bible students consider that Azazel must also be a personal name, but for a being who stands in opposition to God. Others have suggested that Azazel may mean, "sending away," while still others propose that it suggests a locality to which he was dispatched. Gesenius (*Hebrew Lexicon*) observed perceptively that neither an action, nor a region can ever form a natural contrast with Yahweh, only a person can. Azazel must, therefore, be the name of a character whose life and purposes are the opposite of God's.*

*Further, the preposition "for" (*lamed *as a prefix) used with both goats, must be given the same force in each case. If it describes a relationship with a Person called Yahweh, it must also indicate a relationship with a person called Azazel. Almost a century ago Carl Frederich Keil affirmed: "The view that Azazel is the designation of an evil spirit dwelling in the wilderness (Spencer, Rosenmuler, Gesenius) is now almost universally acknowledged" (*Manual of Biblical Archaeology, II, 44). *No valid evidence has appeared during the intervening years to cast a doubt on this conclusion.*[82]

Azazel is not a symbol of Christ; he is a wicked figure. Again, from the *Jewish Encyclopedia:*

Far from involving the recognition of **Azazel** *as a deity, the sending of the goat was, as stated by Nahmanides, a symbolic expression of the idea that the people's sins and their evil consequences were to be sent back to the spirit of desolation and ruin, the source of all impurity. The very fact that the two goats were presented before Yhwh before the one was sacrificed and the other sent into the wilderness, was proof that* **Azazel** *was not ranked with Yhwh, but regarded simply as the personification of* *wickedness in contrast with the righteous government of Yhwh.*[83]

There is an understandable hesitation among some Christians to identify Azazel (the scapegoat) with Satan, because of the suggestion that he somehow shares in the plan of salvation by ultimately bearing away the sins of God's people. This is simply not the case. Christ alone stands as our substitute; only the Lord's goat is sacrificed. The scapegoat sheds its blood for nobody; he is simply removed from the camp of Israel. This is telling us that, in the end, Satan will be made to suffer the consequences for all of the sin and suffering he has caused. He will receive his just deserts for launching a rebellion against God in the first place. He will *not* go free while unrepentant human sinners are required to pay for their sins. The devil will ultimately be destroyed. In a stunning prediction of the devil's ultimate fate, God says this:

"You defiled your sanctuaries by the multitude of your iniquities, By the iniquity of your trading; Therefore I brought fire from your midst; It devoured you, And I turned you to ashes upon the earth In the sight of all who saw you. All who knew you among the peoples are astonished at you; You have become a horror, And shall be no more forever."
(Ezekiel 28:18, 19)

The Feast of Trumpets and the Day of Atonement are an amazing prophecy of last day events. A final warning is issued to planet earth, the judgment convenes, and all decisions are final. For generations, Jewish believers have seen a clear connection between the Day of Atonement rituals and the judgment scene portrayed in the book of Daniel:

I watched till thrones were put in place, and the Ancient of Days was seated; His garment was white as snow, and the hair of His head was like pure wool. His throne was a fiery flame, its wheels a burning fire; a fiery stream issued and came forth from before Him. A thousand thousands ministered to Him; ten thousand times ten thousand stood before Him. The court was seated, and the books were opened." (Daniel 7:9, 10)

In his book on the feasts of Israel, Edward Chumney writes:

Since the court was seated and the books were opened, it is understood to be Rosh Hashanah. *The books are the book of the righteous, the book of the wicked, and the book of remembrance. The third book that will be opened is the book of remembrance (*zikkaron*). This is why the common greeting during* Rosh Hashanah *is "May you be inscribed in the Book of Life."*[84]

The judgment in heaven must take place some time just prior to the Second Coming of Christ. When Jesus returns, all decisions are final:

"He who is unjust, let him be unjust still; he who is filthy, let him be filthy still; he who is righteous, let him be righteous still; he who is holy, let him be holy still. And behold, I am coming quickly, and My reward is with Me, to give to every one according to his work." (Rev. 22:11, 12)

When Christ comes back, it will be too late to change your mind. At that moment your fate will have been sealed for all eternity. All decisions will have been made for all time. There is a vivid warning for us in the Feast of Trumpets and the Day of Atonement: *time will not last forever.* It is possible to put things off until it is simply too late.

And where is *our* warning that the judgment is coming? Many people are surprised to discover that the Bible teaches that the judgment hour is already scheduled. It happens at a definite time predetermined by God:

"...because He has appointed a day on which He will judge the world in righteousness by the Man whom He has ordained. He has given assurance of this to all by raising Him from the dead." (Acts 17:31)

In the early 1800s, as the period of time known as the Dark Ages was just passing into history, there was a sudden explosion in Christian activity. During this time, Bible societies and missionary societies suddenly sprang up all over the planet. Public evangelism and Christian revivals flourished. This period produced some of the greatest preachers and missionaries in Christian history: David Livingstone, Hudson Taylor, Charles Spurgeon, George Muller and Dwight L. Moody.

Not only was the gospel preached with renewed power, a message that had not really been preached for centuries started to spread like wildfire: Jesus is coming soon! Around the globe scores of preachers—independent of each other—started to point to the prophecies of Daniel and Revelation, urging people to come back to Christ before it was too late. One of the most impressive of these movements took root in the United States, where a Baptist minister by the name of William Miller began to preach the soon coming of Jesus Christ. He *did* make the mistake of choosing dates for the Second Coming; however, his message was clear and biblical: the events predicted in Bible prophecy were quickly coming to pass, and the world had entered its final phase of existence.

A quick look at current events—when compared with the prophecies of the Bible—makes it clear that the trumpets have already begun to sound. The rapid pace of global change—wars, disease, and strange weather patterns—paints a clear picture. Time is running out.

In the book of Revelation, we discover that before time completely runs out, a startling message goes out to the world that the judgment hour has already begun:

Then I saw another angel flying in the midst of heaven, having the everlasting gospel to preach to those who dwell on the earth—to every nation, tribe, tongue, and people—saying with a loud voice, "Fear God and give glory to Him, for the hour of His judgment has come; and worship Him who made heaven and earth, the sea and springs of water." (Revelation 14:6, 7)

The final message is not that the judgment *will* come, or that it *is* coming. It says that the judgment *has* come. Is it possible that it is already here?

----

[76] David J. Mitchell, *WAC Bennett and the Rise of British Columbia*, p. 372.
[77] F. C. Gilbert, p. 253
[78] Leviticus 16:8
[79] Leviticus 16:15
[80] The Revised Standard Version renders the verse like this: "...and Aaron shall cast lots upon the two goats, one lot for the LORD and the other lot for Azazel."
[81] *Jewish Encyclopedia,* Azazel. Available at www.jewishencyclopedia.com.
[82] Hardinge, p. 518
[83] *Jewish Encyclopedia,* Azazel.
[84] Bacchiochi, vol 2, p. 60.

CHAPTER THIRTEEN

The Judgment Hour

In the waning days of the Babylonian empire, the prophet Daniel was given a remarkable vision in which he was shown the history of the world in advance. In no uncertain terms, he was told that the collapse of Babylon would give rise to the Medo-Persian Empire,[85] and after that, the Greeks.[86]

Following that, an empire would ravage the world in a way never before seen, with both military means and unprecedented religious corruption. In each instance the angel Gabriel gives Daniel a number of details outlining what each phase of history would bring, with one exception. He does not explain one important part of the vision:

And he said to me, "For two thousand three hundred days;[87] then the sanctuary shall be cleansed." (Daniel 8:14)

Each of the other parts of Daniel's vision was explained in great detail. A ram with uneven horns represents "the kings of Media and Persia." A goat with a notable horn is "the kingdom of Greece." A little horn is described with enough detail that modern Bible scholars have had little trouble identifying it as the Roman Empire, in both its pagan and religious phases. When it comes to the "2,300 days," however, the angel Gabriel leaves us hanging. The information is scant: the vision is *true*, it is to be *sealed up*, and it refers to *many days in the future:*

"And the vision of the evenings and mornings which was told is true;

therefore seal up the vision, for it refers to many days in the future."
(Daniel 8:26)

This explanation does little to satisfy anyone's curiosity. Does that mean we can't understand what God is trying to tell us through the prophecy of the 2,300 days?

Not at all. The prophecies of the Bible are not curiosity pieces devised by God so that angels can amuse themselves as they watch mere mortals try to unravel their meaning. If this prophecy bears such an important place in the prophecies of Daniel, you can be sure we are able to understand it. Furthermore, Jesus explicitly told us that the book of Daniel was written for us to understand:

"Therefore when you see the 'abomination of desolation,' spoken of by Daniel the prophet, standing in the holy place" (whoever reads, let him understand), "then let those who are in Judea flee to the mountains."
(Matthew 24:15, 16)

Jesus urged us to pay attention to the writings of Daniel. He clearly intends for us to understand them. The only problem we face in trying to understand the prophecy of the 2,300 days is that we don't have much information to go on. Fortunately, there are a number of clues in the text of Daniel chapter eight that shed further light on the subject:

Clue One: The vision points to the last days. Gabriel makes this crystal clear:

So he came near where I stood, and when he came I was afraid and fell on my face; but he said to me, "Understand, son of man, that the vision refers to the time of the end." (Daniel 8:17)

Clue Two: It has something to do with an "appointed" time:

And he said, "Look, I am making known to you what shall happen in the latter time of the indignation; for at the appointed time the end shall be." (Daniel 8:19)

Based on what we already know from our study of the sanctuary, this second clue should raise a large red flag in our minds. We have already discovered that there is a time—at the end of time—that has been appointed by God:

"...because He has appointed a day on which He will judge the world in righteousness by the Man whom He has ordained. He has given assurance of this to all by raising Him from the dead." (Acts 17:31)

God has already chosen a day on which to convene heaven's

judgment. According to Paul, this event is as certain as the resurrection of Christ Himself.

Clue Three: The language of Daniel 8 is *sanctuary* language. Both of the animals mentioned (ram, goat) are "clean" animals, and would have been used in the rituals of the sanctuary. Additionally, it mentions daily services and a sanctuary. God is trying to direct our attention to something in the tabernacle.

Clue Four: The language of the vision itself directs us to the sanctuary. In fact, it speaks about the moment when the *sanctuary would be cleansed.* In our last chapter, we have already seen that there was indeed such an event in the annual cycle of festivals celebrated in the sanctuary. On the Day of Atonement, the sanctuary was cleansed of the uncleanness of the children of Israel, [88] and this was understood to be a *day of judgment.*

As the picture in Daniel 8 begins to unfold, it nearly takes your breath away. Other prophecies in Daniel point us unmistakably to the Second Coming of Christ. In Daniel 2, for example, Nebuchadnezzar sees a statue that represents the progression of world empires down through the ages until the moment that God Himself establishes an everlasting kingdom.[89] In Daniel 7 the same progression of kingdoms is given again, but this time leading down through successive world empires until heaven's judgment hour begins. In Daniel 8 we find another progression of kingdoms: Medo-Persia, Greece, Rome (united and divided), and then an event that is described as the *cleansing of the sanctuary.* We have already learned that the Old Testament cleansing of the sanctuary represented the judgment in heaven.

What is truly spectacular is that this prophecy is revealing a *date.* It doesn't simply suggest that the judgment begins at some remote point in the future; it is *very* specific. It tells us that there will be 2,300 days until it begins.

It can't possibly mean 2,300 literal days from the moment Daniel received the vision, however. If that were the case, it would mean that the final judgment hour began before Christ came to earth the first time—and that simply doesn't make sense. So what *does* it mean?

It is remarkably easy to figure out. In Bible prophecy (and in prophecy alone), a day is symbolic of a year. This principle is easy to see in other prophetic passages:

"According to the number of the days in which you spied out the land, forty days, for each day you shall bear your guilt one year, namely forty years, and you shall know My rejection." (Numbers 14:34)

"And when you have completed them, lie again on your right side; then you shall bear the iniquity of the house of Judah forty days. I have laid on you a day for each year." (Ezekiel 4:6)

A prophecy of 2,300 *days* represents a period of 2,300 years. A span of more than 2,000 years makes much more sense in light of the fact that we are talking about a last-day event. The only question that remains to be answered is *when* this period of time begins? Gabriel gives no clear reference points, and if we don't know when the prophecy begins, we can't figure out when it ends.

When you keep reading, however, you make a remarkable discovery. At the end of chapter 8, Daniel is confused and does not understand what he has just heard. He understood the ram, the goat, and the little horn, but the 2,300 days were still a mystery:

And I, Daniel, fainted and was sick for days; afterward I arose and went about the king's business. I was astonished by the vision, but no one understood it. (Daniel 8:27)

That is the end of the chapter, but it's not the end of the story! In the very next chapter, we find that Babylon has collapsed and Darius the Mede is now reigning over the former Babylonian empire. Daniel is pouring over the prophecies of Jeremiah, wondering when his people might expect to return to the Promised Land—and then Gabriel suddenly returns with an important message:

Now while I was speaking, praying, and confessing my sin and the sin of my people Israel, and presenting my supplication before the LORD my God for the holy mountain of my God, yes, while I was speaking in prayer, the man Gabriel, whom I had seen in the vision at the beginning, being caused to fly swiftly, reached me about the time of the evening offering. And he informed me, and talked with me, and said, "O Daniel, I have now come forth to give you skill to understand. At the beginning of your supplications the command went out, and I have come to tell you, for you are greatly beloved; therefore consider the matter, and understand the vision." (Daniel 8:20-23)

It is important to pay careful attention to the details in this passage. Gabriel—the same angel that Daniel had seen in the "vision at the beginning"—has now come to help Daniel understand "the vision." What vision is he talking about? The one that Daniel previously hadn't understood—the vision of the 2300 days.

Then Gabriel gives Daniel some information that unlocks the whole prophecy:

"Seventy weeks are determined for your people and for your holy city, to finish the transgression, to make an end of sins, to make reconciliation for iniquity, to bring in everlasting righteousness, to seal up vision and prophecy, and to anoint the Most Holy. Know therefore and understand, that from the going forth of the command to restore and build Jerusalem until Messiah the Prince, there shall be seven weeks and sixty-two weeks; the street shall be built again, and the wall, even in troublesome times. And after the sixty-two weeks Messiah shall be cut off, but not for Himself; and the people of the prince who is to come shall destroy the city and the sanctuary. The end of it shall be with a flood, and till the end of the war desolations are determined. Then he shall confirm a covenant with many for one week; but in the middle of the week He shall bring an end to sacrifice and offering. And on the wing of abominations shall be one who makes desolate, even until the consummation, which is determined, is poured out on the desolate." (Daniel 9:24-27)

This passage is known as the "70-week" prophecy because of the reference to that period of time in the opening verses. We need to examine it carefully, not only because it is one of the most striking prophecies in the Bible, but also because it is one of the most widely misunderstood. And when we have finished studying, it will prove to be the key that unlocks the mysterious prophecy of the 2,300 days.[90]

The angel Gabriel begins by informing Daniel that "70 weeks" are determined for his people. The word "determined" (Hebrew *chathak*, "divide, cut") is probably better translated "cut off." This is a reference back to the 2,300-day prophecy from Daniel chapter 8. Gabriel is simply breaking it down for easier understanding. "Here, Daniel," he says, "I'm going to break off a seventy-week portion of that prophecy to make it easier for you to understand."

The "70 weeks" are set aside, or cut off, for Daniel's people. Who are Daniel's people? The Jews. This prophecy sets aside a specific period of time for the nation of Israel. Remember that in Bible prophecy, a *day* is used to represent a *year*. Seventy weeks, or 490 days, is a period of 490 literal years. The period of time specifically set aside in this prophecy for the nation of Israel is therefore 490 years:

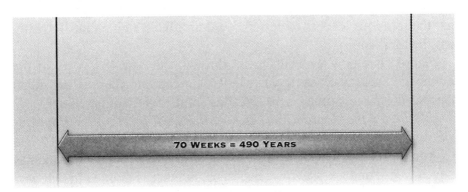

On its own, this information is of little value, because we have no idea when this period of time begins or ends. Fortunately, Gabriel provides a few more details:

"...from the going forth of the command to restore and build Jerusalem until Messiah the Prince, there shall be seven weeks and sixty-two weeks..." (Daniel 9:25)

Daniel is told there will be a total of 69 weeks (7 weeks + 62 weeks = 69 weeks) from the time that a decree is given to rebuild the city of Jerusalem until the Messiah appears. Using the day-for-a-year principle, we discover that this is a period of 483 literal years.

After the fall of Babylon, there were four decrees given by Persian kings for the Israelites to return to their homeland and rebuild the city of Jerusalem.

The first two decrees, recorded in the Old Testament book of Ezra, were given in the years 537 B.C. and 520 B.C., respectively. Both of these decrees failed to accomplish anything significant. The third decree, however, given by Artaxerxes in 457 B.C., was different. It made the rebuilding of Jerusalem a reality. Not only did Artaxerxes issue the decree, he also helped to finance the project![91]

The decree of Artaxerxes, given in 457 B.C., is the starting point for the prophecy. Gabriel promised Daniel that 483 years after this decree, the Messiah would appear. That brings us to the year 27 A.D.[92] According to Luke 3:1, Jesus was baptized in the "fifteenth year of Tiberius Caesar," which was 27 A.D. At the Jordan River, God the Father publicly announced Jesus as His Son, and the Holy Spirit anointed Him. Immediately following His baptism, Jesus began His public ministry.[93]

Given the remarkable accuracy of the prophecy, it is incomprehensible that the religious leaders of Jesus' day didn't have a clue that He really *was* the Messiah!

Gabriel has now walked Daniel through the first 483 years of the prophecy. There are seven years left over, or *one final week*. What happens during this time? Verse 26 adds some important details:

"And after the sixty-two weeks Messiah shall be cut off, but not for Himself." (Daniel 9:26)

You will remember that the 69 weeks in verse 25 were described as "seven weeks and sixty-two weeks." That number is divided in that way for an important reason. Seven weeks would be 49 years, ending in 408 B.C. That was the year that the rebuilding of Jerusalem was completed. For the next 62 years, Israel waited for Messiah to come.

The 62 weeks ended in 27 A.D. with the appearance of Jesus as Messiah. Gabriel tells us that *after* the 62-week waiting period, Messiah would be "cut off," but not for Himself. This happened when Jesus was crucified in the spring of 31 A.D., after three and a half years of public ministry.

There is a second reference to the crucifixion in this prophecy, found in verse 27:

"Then he shall confirm a covenant with many for one week; but in the middle of the week He shall bring an end to sacrifice and offering..." (Daniel 9:27)

This is one of the most critical verses in the prophecy. Christ would confirm a covenant for "one week"—which is the period of time left over when the first 69 weeks came to a close in 27 A.D. In the middle of this "week"—a period of seven years—He would put an end to sacrifices and offerings.

The death of Christ put an end to the sacrificial system, which had sacrificed countless lambs in anticipation of the "Lamb of God, who takes away the sin of the world." Once Christ died for us on the cross, the sacrificial system was no longer necessary, and thus His death brought an end to "sacrifice and offering."

Amazingly, the crucifixion took place after three and a half years of ministry, *exactly in the middle of the last week of Daniel's prophecy:*

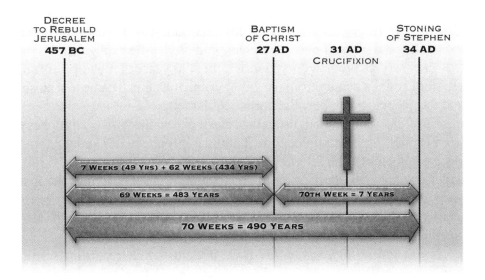

All of the details fit Daniel's seventy-week prophecy. Some, however, have asked the question: *If Christ died after three and a half years, how could He be said to confirm a covenant for one week, or a period of seven years?* The answer is simple. Don't forget that the entire period of 490 years was "cut off" or set aside for Daniel's people, the Jews. Christ's disciples—empowered by the Holy Spirit—continued to minister to the nation of Israel for another three and a half years after Christ died. Their additional three-and-a-half-year ministry completes the prophecy, and the seventieth week comes to its conclusion in 34 A.D. (The complete prophecy,[94] remarkable for its breathtaking precision, looks like the diagram above.)

Did anything significant happen in 34 A.D.? Absolutely. That year, the religious authorities stoned a deacon named Stephen to death. In the seventh chapter of Acts, Stephen preaches a final message of mercy to the leaders of Israel, recounting how God had painstakingly worked with their nation over the centuries. At the close of his sermon, the outraged rulers killed him. Subsequently, the Christian church was threatened with intense persecution by a young man named Saul, who had been present at Stephen's execution. As a result of Saul's devastating harassments against the early church, the believers were forced to scatter across the globe.

The natural side effect of this mass dispersion was that the gospel also went to the Gentile world. In fact, through a series of miraculous incidents, Saul himself became a champion of Gentile evangelism!

Precisely as predicted by Gabriel, the 490 years that had been "cut off" for Daniel's people from the 2,300 years of Daniel 8 came to a close, and the gospel spread past the borders of Israel.

Now that we have all of the details that make up the 70-week prophecy from Daniel 9, we can unlock the 2,300-day prophecy of Daniel 8 quite easily. Remember, the 70-week prophecy was "cut off" from the 2,300-day prophecy, making it easier to understand. Gabriel describes the first portion of the 2,300-day prophecy to Daniel by giving him the details of its first 490 years. Those 490 years began in 457 B.C.—which also becomes the starting date for the 2,300 years of Daniel 8:14.

If you add 2,300 years to 457 B.C., it yields a rather startling result. You arrive at the date 1844 A.D.—*a date that has already come and gone.* In that year, the work of "cleansing the sanctuary" in heaven began. *We are now living in earth's last hour.* We shouldn't be surprised. Remember that at some point just prior to Christ's return, the message goes to the world that the judgment hour has already begun:

Then I saw another angel flying in the midst of heaven, having the everlasting gospel to preach to those who dwell on the earth—to every nation, tribe, tongue, and people—saying with a loud voice, "Fear God and give glory to Him, for the hour of His judgment has come; and worship Him who made heaven and earth, the sea and springs of water." (Revelation 14:6, 7)

That very message is already circling the globe. Every year, millions of people discover that we are living in the final moments of earth's history. The judgment hour in heaven is already under way, and Jesus will soon be here.

When you study the feasts of Israel, it is important to notice a deliberate pattern. The early festivals—like the Passover and Firstfruits—give us a breathtaking prophecy of Christ's work at the cross and His resurrection. The feast of Pentecost shows us the beginning of His work in Heaven's sanctuary, complete with the anointing of His church below with the Holy Spirit. The work of leading sinners to the throne of grace thus goes on for centuries—until the trumpets are blown and the warning goes out that time is running out.

The fall feasts give us a picture of how Christ wraps up His work in heaven's sanctuary and prepares for the Second Coming. The feast of trumpets was a loud warning to the world, preparing them for the judgment hour. As the Christian church came out of the Dark Ages, it began just such a warning to the world: *Jesus is coming soon.*

Then, before Christ comes back, the heavenly judgment convenes, and a period of deep soul-searching among God's people begins. The High Priest makes His final approach to the mercy seat in the Most Holy Place; when He is finished presenting His blood there, time will be over, and those who refused to make things right with God will be cut off from His presence forever.

The timeline of the sanctuary services gives us a broad picture of Christian history, from the cross to the judgment hour. At this moment of history we find ourselves living in, there is just one more feast to go: the Feast of Tabernacles.

---

[85] Daniel 8:20

[86] Daniel 8:21

[87] Literally, "two thousand evening mornings." In Biblical understanding, days were reckoned from sunset to sunset, placing the dark part of the day first. This is why, in the book of Genesis, we are told that "evening and morning were the first day, " etc. This is why this same vision is referred to as the vision of "evenings and mornings" in verse 26. (continued on page 125)

[88] Leviticus 23:27-32; 16:16

[89] For more details, see *The Appearing*.

[90] The material I'm about to present will get a little bit technical for many readers; however, I encourage you to stick with it, because it's going to prove important for an understanding of last-day events. It may help to chart each step on a piece of paper as we go. I think if you do that, you'll discover this isn't nearly as tough to understand as some people would have you believe.

[91] See Ezra 7:11-26 for details.

[92] If you're doing the math, you'll discover that adding 483 years to 457 B.C. brings you to 26 A.D. Remember, however, that there was no such thing as a "zero" year, so when you cross the B.C./A.D. line, you need to add one to your total. This takes us to 27 A.D.

[93] Luke 3:22, 23

[94] There are some who have taken the final week of this prophecy and removed it from the rest, placing it at the end of time. There is nothing in the text to warrant this. For a detailed analysis of the seventy-week prophecy, see chapter six of *The Appearing*.

CHAPTER FOURTEEN

Home at Last

When the service of the solemn judgment hour in Israel had passed for another year, it gave way to the highlight of all festivals: the *Feast of Tabernacles*. Little huts made of branches blanketed the city of Jerusalem, spilling outside its gates into the surrounding countryside. As with some of the other feasts, the Feast of Tabernacles took place at harvest time, so it was a cause for great celebration. Plump, juicy grapes were ready for picking, and the olives were ready for the presses. Everyone was jubilant that there would be adequate provisions for the year ahead.

The Feast of Tabernacles was not just a celebration of God's goodness to Israel for that specific year; it was also a tribute to God's provision for them during the years they lived in tents as they made their way from Egypt to the Promised Land. It was a celebration of the fact that God had been faithful in His promise to bring them to Canaan, and that they now found themselves in His presence in the Land of Promise.

If Abraham had still been alive when the Feast of Tabernacles was instituted, it would have brought him a lot of satisfaction. God had promised that his descendants—millions of them—would inherit the land of Canaan. He had chosen to give up the comforts of Chaldea and live in tents to follow God in faith. The Feast of Tabernacles was a celebration that, even though it may have caused temporary inconvenience and discomfort to follow God, He *always* makes good on His word.

However, the earthly land of Canaan was not Abraham's ultimate hope, as we have already discovered in an earlier chapter:

By faith Abraham obeyed when he was called to go out to the place which he would receive as an inheritance. And he went out, not knowing where he was going. By faith he dwelt in the land of promise as in a foreign country, dwelling in tents with Isaac and Jacob, the heirs with him of the same promise; for he waited for the city which has foundations, whose builder and maker is God. (Hebrews 11:8-10)

The promise made to Abraham really has a dual fulfillment. His literal genetic descendants, the Israelites, inherited the literal land of Canaan. The Feast of Tabernacles was a celebration of that fact. But the *spiritual* descendants of Abraham—those who have "put on Christ"—are looking to inherit the *spiritual* Promised Land:

For as many of you as were baptized into Christ have put on Christ. There is neither Jew nor Greek, there is neither slave nor free, there is neither male nor female; for you are all one in Christ Jesus. And if you are Christ's, then you are Abraham's seed, and heirs according to the promise. (Galatians 3:27-29)

The 70-week prophecy given to Daniel proves something very important. Those 70 weeks, or 490 years, were "cut off" for Daniel's people, the Jews. After that time, the gospel went to the Gentile world, an event marked by the stoning of Stephen. The literal nation of Israel no longer functioned as God's chosen people. The gospel was taken from them and given to the *spiritual* nation of Israel, made up of believers from all walks of life.

In the twenty-first chapter of Matthew, Jesus tells a remarkable parable in which God's kingdom is compared to a vineyard. The ancient Israelites were chosen as vinedressers to work in the vineyard, but they were found to be unfaithful. When God sent messengers to collect the fruits that rightfully belonged to Him, His messengers—one after the other—were either beaten or killed. That is when God decided to send His Son:

"Then last of all he sent his son to them, saying, 'They will respect my son.' But when the vinedressers saw the son, they said among themselves, 'This is the heir. Come, let us kill him and seize his inheritance.' So they took him and cast him out of the vineyard and killed him. Therefore, when the owner of the vineyard comes, what will he do to those vinedressers?"

They said to Him, "He will destroy those wicked men miserably, and lease his vineyard to other vinedressers who will render to him the fruits in their seasons." (Matthew 21:37-41)

Jesus' audience was quick to understand the story and assess the situation: naturally, if the keepers of the vineyard were found unfaithful, they should be removed and replaced by someone more dependable. And indeed, that is exactly what Jesus predicted would happen to the nation of Israel:

"Therefore I say to you, the kingdom of God will be taken from you and given to a nation bearing the fruits of it." Matthew 21:43

After the crucifixion of Jesus, the period of probation for literal Israel quickly drew to a close. After Daniel's 490-year prophecy was fulfilled, literal Israel was supplanted by *spiritual* Israel—a special group of Abraham's spiritual ancestors, made up of both Jews and Gentiles.

This is very important to remember when studying Bible prophecy. In the Old Testament, you had two literal cities: Babylon and Jerusalem. In the New Testament, these cities are used as symbols for two groups of people living in the last days: spiritual Babylon and spiritual Israel. One group is content to remain part of this world; the other group is waiting for its inheritance from God. Not only did the Feast of Tabernacles point back to the conquest of literal Canaan, it also pointed forward to the heavenly city that was promised to Abraham and his descendants. The little huts they lived in during the festival were designed to make the Israelites homesick for heaven. They were a reminder that this earth is not our final home. It is just a "tent" that we are living in until we arrive in the heavenly Promised Land.

The story is told of a tourist who happened to visit a rabbi in his home. He noticed that the rabbi lived very simply; his home consisted of only one room with some books, a table and a bench. He looked around the room in amazement, and couldn't help but ask, "Rabbi, where is your furniture?"

The rabbi looked around the room for a moment and then said, "And where is *your* furniture?"

The tourist was surprised by the response. "But rabbi, I don't need any furniture, because I don't live here!"

"Well," said the wise teacher, "I don't either. I'm just passing through."

It is important for us to remember that we don't really belong here—at least not forever. This world is not our final home. The huts at the Feast of Tabernacles were not permanent structures because they were designed to teach us that, like the Israelites on the way to Canaan, we are only passing through this world on our way to the Heavenly Promised Land.

Before Jesus left for heaven to begin His ministry in the heavenly sanctuary, He emphasized God's promise that there is a heavenly city for us to inherit:

"Let not your heart be troubled; you believe in God, believe also in Me. In My Father's house are many mansions; if it were not so, I would have told you. I go to prepare a place for you. And if I go and prepare a place for you, I will come again and receive you to Myself; that where I am, there you may be also." (John 14:1-3)

In the last book of the Bible, John is shown the heavenly city that belongs to Abraham's spiritual descendants—those who place their trust in Christ:

Now I saw a new heaven and a new earth, for the first heaven and the first earth had passed away. Also there was no more sea. Then I, John, saw the holy city, New Jerusalem, coming down out of heaven from God, prepared as a bride adorned for her husband. And I heard a loud voice from heaven saying, "Behold, the tabernacle of God is with men, and He will dwell with them, and they shall be His people. God Himself will be with them and be their God. And God will wipe away every tear from their eyes; there shall be no more death, nor sorrow, nor crying. There shall be no more pain, for the former things have passed away." Then He who sat on the throne said, "Behold, I make all things new." And He said to me, "Write, for these words are true and faithful." (Revelation 21:1-5)

The deepest desire in the heart of God is to place His presence among His people. In the end, after sin and suffering have been eliminated for all time, He will take up residence among us forever. Thanks to the gift of Calvary, the barrier caused by sin will be eliminated and we can once again dwell forever in the presence of God.

The Feast of Tabernacles was the last feast of the Israelite religious year, and of all the feasts, it is the only one that has not yet met its fulfillment in Christ. The heavenly judgment hour is under way right now, and when that is finished, Christ will return for His people. Then we will "tabernacle" with Him forever.

It is interesting that this final feast was also known as the *Feast of Ingathering,* because it took place in conjunction with the final harvest of the year. This is a specific prophecy of the Second Coming, which is why Jesus often referred to the end of the world and the Second Coming as a "harvest."

God's desire to place His presence among us is also evident when you compare the ancient tabernacle in the camp of Israel and the description of the New Jerusalem in the book of Revelation:

And he carried me away in the Spirit to a great and high mountain, and showed me the great city, the holy Jerusalem, descending out of heaven from God, having the glory of God. Her light was like a most precious stone, like a jasper stone, clear as crystal. Also she had a great and high wall with twelve gates, and twelve angels at the gates, and names written on them, which are the names of the twelve tribes of the children of Israel: three gates on the east, three gates on the north, three gates on the south, and three gates on the west. Now the wall of the city had twelve foundations, and on them were the names of the twelve apostles of the Lamb. And he who talked with me had a gold reed to measure the city, its gates, and its wall. The city is laid out as a square; its length is as great as its breadth. And he measured the city with the reed: twelve thousand furlongs. Its length, breadth, and height are equal. (Revelation 21:10-16)

There are a few details in this passage that are really interesting. First of all, there are 12 gates to the city—three on each side. Above each gate is written the name of one of the 12 tribes of Israel. Compare this information with a description of the camp of Israel found in the second chapter of Numbers, and you will discover that precisely three tribes of Israelites camped on each side of the tabernacle.

Furthermore, the proportions of the Holy City are equal in all three dimensions. It is a perfect cube. The same is true of the Most Holy Place in the Old Testament tabernacle, the place where the presence of God was manifested above the Ark—it was 15 feet wide, deep and high.[95] The camp of Israel says something important about heaven: Israel used to have to camp *around* the throne of God, separated from Him by a thick veil.

In the New Jerusalem, there are gates on all four sides leading straight into the presence of God inside the city. The separation caused by sin is now over. Through the blood of Christ, we have the liberty of entering into the presence of God.

The remarkable parallels between the Most Holy Place of the wilderness tabernacle and the Holy City are unmistakable. God is trying to tell us something important: *His deepest desire has always been to dwell among His people.* Our fall into sin and rebellion didn't diminish His love for us. The sanctuary was a picture of His ultimate goal—His people in His presence forever. The rituals that took place inside that sanctuary showed us how He planned to make it happen—through the atoning work of Jesus Christ.

A careful study of the Bible shows us that God's Presence has always been closer than we think. He placed His unmistakable Presence at the gates of the Garden of Eden so that we could see that He had a plan in place to solve the problems we had created through sin and rebellion. He sealed His covenant with Abraham by His fiery Presence so that we could know that in the darkest night of sin, we still had a loving Heavenly Father who would one day bring us into the heavenly Promised Land. He showed Himself to Moses in the burning bush to help usrealize the power that is available as we press on towards the kingdom.

He led the Israelites by His presence in a pillar of cloud by day, shielding them from the heat of the sun as they crossed the wilderness in pursuit of their inheritance. At night He manifested Himself as a pillar of fire, providing them light in the darkness. When they pitched camp, He took up residence in the midst of their camp, and walked among His people.[96] When the Israelites took up residence in the land of promise and built a permanent temple, God filled it with His glorious presence.[97]

After the Babylonian captivity He gave the Israelites a new temple, then blessed it in an unusual way by coming as a human being and teaching publicly within its precincts. At His death, the veil in the temple was torn in two, forever sealing the fact that the earthly sanctuary had served its purpose. Then, after ascending into heaven, Jesus sent the Holy Spirit to establish His permanent presence among the members of His church. And now, as the church on earth carries the good news of the cross to the far corners of the earth, Jesus serves as our High Priest in heaven's sanctuary.

The feasts of the ancient tabernacle present a divine timeline of events, carrying us from the death of Christ straight through to the Second Coming. The Passover demonstrates to us the Lamb of God who gave His life for the sins of the world, and invites us to sprinkle His atoning blood on the doorposts of our hearts. The Feast of Firstfruits shows us a Savior who is triumphant over the grave, and holds out to us the promise that we, too, will have victory over the grave when Jesus returns in glory. The Feast of Pentecost was a harvest festival; 3,000 were reaped for the kingdom in a single day as the Christian church began its Spirit-led work. Through the work of the church, the tangible presence of God continued on earth.

The Feast of Trumpets gives us a warning that time will quickly run out, and the Day of Atonement signals the final judgment hour. The only festival yet to be fulfilled is the Feast of Tabernacles, when God takes up residence with His redeemed people for all eternity.

There is a day quickly approaching when the last funeral will have been conducted, the last tear will be shed, and the last hospital will be closed permanently. This world is not our home; there is nothing here worth clinging to when we realize that God is about to restore us to His presence. A million years from now, as we stand in Paradise, we will hardly be able to remember this world.

Perhaps the greatest tragedy in the universe is the fact that in spite of the abundant evidence God has presented to prove that He has a plan to save us, so many still choose to make their way through life following their own plan. Consider, for a moment, the stunning precision with which the sanctuary services predicted the life and ministry of Christ. Calculate the odds—if you can—that the predictions made in the sanctuary would all come to pass with such remarkable accuracy. Clearly, God has a plan that has never yet failed.

At this moment, it is only a matter of time before the final pieces of the prophecy fall into place. In light of the fact that not one detail of the sanctuary prophecy has failed to this point, you can be sure that the final details will also come to pass with stunning precision. Jesus really *will* come again—and that moment, like His presence, is a lot closer than you think.

If you only take one thing away from your study of the sanctuary, I pray that it will be this: God has taken every measure possible to ensure that you are ready for Jesus to come. His plan for your salvation is not haphazard; He has taken care of absolutely every detail. The only detail that might still be missing at this moment is your decision.

The gift of Christ at the cross is not automatically applied to you. God is not in the business of forcing people to follow Him. Those who will be in the presence of God for all eternity will be there because they *want* to be there.

The question you face, as you finish reading this book, is simple. Have you made your decision? The only hope you have is the blood of Christ. You will not get to heaven on your own merit. You need Him desperately. And right now, as you prepare to put this book down, His voice is speaking to your heart. This is *your* moment to encounter the presence of God. The Lamb of God is asking for your heart. What is your answer?

---

[95] See the dimensions of the tabernacle as given in Exodus 26:1-34. You arrive at 15 feet by counting each cubit as 18 inches, a commonly accepted interpretation of this biblical measurement.
[96] See Deuteronomy 23:14
[97] 2 Chronicles 7:1, 2

Bibliography

Andreasen, M. L. *The Sanctuary Service*. Hagerstown, MD: Review and Herald Publishing Association, 1947.

Bacchiocchi, Samuele. *God's Festivals in Scripture and History*. Berrien Springs, MI: Biblical Perspectives, 1995.

Boonstra, Shawn. *O Jerusalem, Jerusalem!* Oshawa: It Is Written Canada, 2001.

Clarke, Adam. *The Holy Bible: A Commentary and Critical Notes*. Nashville: Abingdon, n.d.

D'Aubigne, J. H. Merle. *History of the Reformation of the Sixteenth Century*. Grand Rapids: Baker Book House, 1987.

Gilbert, F. C. *Practical Lessons from the Experience of Israel for the Church Today*. South Lancaster, Mass.: South Lancaster Printing Company, 1902.

Hardinge, Leslie. *With Jesus in His Sanctuary*. Harrisburg, PA: American Cassette Ministries, 1991.

Haskell, Stephen. *The Cross and Its Shadow*. South Lancaster, Mass.: South Lancaster Printing Company, 1914.

Herodotus. *The Histories*. New York: Penguin Classics, 1976.

LaHaye, Tim and Jerry B. Jenkins. *Are We Living in the End Times?* Wheaton, Illinois: Tyndale House Publishers, 1999.

Livio, Mario. *The Golden Ratio: The Story of Phi, the World's Most Astonishing Number*. New York: Broadway Books, 2003.

Matthews, Victor. *Old Testament Turning Points: The Narratives that Shaped a Nation*. Grand Rapids, Michigan: Baker Academic, 2005.

Mitchell, David J. *WAC Bennett and the Rise of British Columbia*. Vancouver: Douglas & McIntyre, 1983.

Von Daniken, Erich. *Chariots of the Gods?* Toronto: Bantam Books, 1971.

Discover Answers
to life's
Questions

Bibleinfo.com
offers answers to hundreds of
everyday questions. Discover
what the Bible has to say
about your question. The
answer is only a click away!

KidsBibleinfo.com™
big answers for little people℠

Plus, there is a fun, educational
and inspirational site designed
for children. Explore interactive
games, Bible lessons, character-
building stories and more at
www.KidsBibleinfo.com.

Bibleinfo.com®

Bible answers to hundreds of life's questions in 17 languages.